Jira Work Management for Business Teams

Accelerate digital transformation and modernize
your organization with Jira Work Management

John Funk

BIRMINGHAM—MUMBAI

Jira Work Management for Business Teams

Copyright © 2022 Packt Publishing

Group Product Manager: Alok Dhuri

Publishing Product Manager: Shweta Bairoliya

Senior Editors: Storm Mann and Nisha Cleetus

Content Development Editor: Nithya Sadanandan

Technical Editor: Pradeep Sahu

Copy Editor: Safis Editing

Project Coordinator: Deeksha Thakkar

Proofreader: Safis Editing

Indexer: Manju Arasan

Production Designer: Vijay Kamble

Marketing Coordinator: Deepak Kumar

First published: January 2022

Production reference: 1231221

Published by Packt Publishing Ltd.
Livery Place
35 Livery Street
Birmingham
B3 2PB, UK.

ISBN 978-1-80323-200-3

www.packt.com

This book is dedicated to my partner and best friend – my wife, Suzanne. And to my two boys, Jonathan and Jeffrey, of whom I am overly proud for the young men you have grown up to be.

– John Funk

Contributors

About the author

John Funk is an Agile Tools Administrator with Ramsey Solutions. He is highly skilled in project management and Jira administration in the media and publishing domains. John has more than 25 years of experience in project management across US Government and commercial projects, as well as time spent in South America. He holds a B.S. in secondary education and multiple Atlassian Jira certifications.

John values his contribution and service as an Atlassian community leader and has participated in several Jira Early Adoption Program (EAP) teams, including the Jira Work Management EAP. He was also one of the first Atlassian Certification Acceleration Experience group leaders, helping to prepare professionals to pass the ACP-120 certification exam.

About the reviewer

Shane Fender is an IT professional with more than 10 years of experience in various software and technology companies. An IT community leader, he co-founded the SpiceCorps of Silicon Valley group to connect IT pros and introduce the community to upcoming technology companies. As a thought leader, he is often sought as a speaker or panelist for various marketing and product events. He believes that the distance between IT product teams and IT professionals will continue to shrink as the industry continues to advance. His technical skills include Python, PowerShell, Okta, Onelogin, Atlassian suite, Office 365, and Google Workspace. Shane is enthusiastic and curious and is always interested in learning something new.

Table of Contents

Preface

Section 1: Jira Work Management Basics

1

Why Choose Jira Work Management?

Technical requirements	4	Review of the Jira Core product	12
Comparing project types in Jira	5	What's new in JWM?	12
JWM projects	7	New terms learned	
JSW projects	8	in this chapter	14
JSM projects	11	Summary	15

2

Working with Project Templates

Technical requirements	18	Recruitment	30
What are JWM templates?	18	New Employee Onboarding	31
How are JVM templates grouped?	19	Performance Review	32
		Lead Tracking	33
Exploring the information		Procurement	34
available for templates	22	Sales Pipeline	35
Issue types, workflow, and board		Email Campaign	36
relationships	22	Budget Creation	37
How to read a workflow	23	Personal Task Planner	38
Project Management	25		
Task Tracking	26	Deciding which template to use	39
Content Management	27	New terms learned in	
Document Approval	28	this chapter	39
Web Design Process	29	Summary	40

3
Creating Your First Project

Technical requirements	42	Project details	54
Let's create a project!	42	People	56
The project board	46	Issue types	56
The project has been		Screen and issue layout	57
created – now what?	47	Schemes	62
Back to the board	52		
		New terms learned	
Accessing the Jira Work		**in this chapter**	**64**
Management Administration		**Summary**	**64**
components	**53**		

Section 2: Enhancing Your JWM Project

4
Modifying the Board, Workflow, and Associated Schemes

Technical requirements	68	The schemes used	
Using the board	68	by JWM projects	91
Finding the board	69	**Working with Atlassian**	
Components of the board	70	**Marketplace apps**	**94**
Functions of the board	72	Jira Miscellaneous Workflow	
Creating a second board	73	Extensions by Innovalog	
		Atlassian Apps	95
Accessing and modifying		ScriptRunner for Jira by Adaptavist	95
the workflow	**75**	Other apps	96
The workflow text view	77		
The workflow diagram view	80	**New terms learned**	
The workflow edit mode	81	**in this chapter**	**96**
Editing the workflow	82	**Summary**	**96**
Adding statuses	87		

5

JWM Toolset: Summary, List, Timeline, and the Calendar

Technical requirements	100	Filtering issues	112
The features of JWM	100	Sorting issues	113
Issues and their relationships to the JWM features	102	Working with the Timeline	113
JWM Summary section	103	Changing durations	114
Activity	104	Dependencies	115
Statistics	106	Timeline filters	116
		Exporting a timeline	116
Using the List	107	Sharing a timeline	117
Changing columns	109	Adding issues to the Calendar	117
Changing the order of columns	110	New terms learned in this chapter	120
Resizing columns	110		
Inline editing	111	Summary	120

6

Forms, Issues, Dashboards, and Reports

Technical requirements	122	Accessing and using reports	132
Creating forms	122	Creating simple filters	134
Creating a form	123	Saving a filter	137
Adding fields to a form	124		
Adding a description for a form	126	Implementing dashboards and incorporating gadgets	140
Required fields and changing field labels	126	New terms learned in this chapter	145
Previewing a form	128		
Sharing a form	129	Summary	145
Viewing issues	130		

7

Managing Fields, Screens, and Issue Layouts

Technical requirements	148	How issue layouts affect the fields on your screens	160
Creating and using custom fields	148	Screen schemes	162
Adding fields to screens	152	New terms learned in this chapter	164
Editing the context for a custom field	153		
Using screens to view and edit your work	156	Summary	164

Section 3: Administering Jira Work Management Projects

8

Configuring Permissions and Simple Administration

Technical requirements	168	JWM project administrator capabilities	190
User management	168		
User list	172	Jira administrators versus project administrators	190
Project roles and permissions	176	New terms learned in this chapter	191
Configuring the permission scheme	180		
Permission helper	182	Summary	192
Applying issue-level security	184		

9
Duplicating Projects and Starting Outside the Box

Technical requirements	194	Migrating existing Jira projects to Jira Work Management	204
Creating a project based on an existing project	194	Working with Marketplace apps – Deep Clone for Jira	206
Using shared schemes	199	Summary	208
Creating issues externally	203		

10
Using Project Automation

Technical requirements	210	Automation rule executions and usage limitations	224
What is automation?	210		
Creating automation rules	212	New terms learned in this chapter	225
Using automation templates	219	Summary	225
Common automation use cases	222	Further reading	226

Index

Other Books You May Enjoy

Preface

Learning a new tool can be very daunting, especially software surrounding what often feels like the mystique of project management. But Atlassian has cleared much of the mystery of getting started with a revamp of its initial Jira Core offering for the cloud.

This step-by-step, hands-on book will help you create your first project in practically no time and with little effort. You can even get started with Jira and manage your project with up to 10 users for free. But don't let that fool you, the Jira Work Management (JWM) product is full of surprising power yet simple features that even novices can use immediately.

By the end of this book, you will be up and running with your first Jira Work Management project already created and probably some initial tasks as well. You'll understand how to do the simple things needed to administer your project and keep it functioning properly.

All of this and more in an easy browser-based tool provided by Atlassian, one of the world's leaders in project management software. Take a peek inside and let's get started!

Who this book is for

This book is for product and project managers who want to learn how to quickly get started with non-software projects in Jira. End users working as part of functional teams such as HR, finance, legal, marketing, and so on will also benefit greatly. Familiarity with Jira is helpful but not required.

What this book covers

This book is a treasure trove for someone new to Jira. It is one of the best ways to get started with one of the most used and most powerful project management tools in the world. Each chapter walks you step by step through the key concepts and functionality of the tool.

Chapter 1, Why Choose Jira Work Management?, covers the concepts of Jira Work Management projects, including their principal use and for which situations they are best suited. This chapter compares the various Jira project types and their structures and how to determine the best case to use for your situation. It also describes the differences in the products to help ease the move into the next generation of the tool.

Chapter 2, Working with Project Templates, covers the use of templates in creating Jira Work Management projects. There are many classifications or groupings of templates in Jira Work Management. This chapter also explores the differences between each of the available templates and the underlying components.

Chapter 3, Creating Your First Project, covers the nuts and bolts of creating a new project. It begins by piggybacking on the templates discussion from *Chapter 2* and ends with you completing your first project with the insights learned.

Chapter 4, Modifying the Board, Workflow, and Associated Schemes, covers how the creation of a project creates the initial board, workflow, and associated schemes. It also covers how to modify the board and workflow and the factors that should be considered when making those changes. Finally, the chapter shows how shared schemes can be updated.

Chapter 5, JWM Toolset: Summary, List, Timeline, and the Calendar, introduces the newest features of Jira Work Management. It walks through the set of tools provided in the product, including the function of the Summary section, List, Timeline, and the in-project calendar. As these are the features that set JWM projects apart from all other projects, the chapter delves into the workings of each tool.

Chapter 6, Forms, Issues, Dashboards, and Reports, guides you through the creation of simple Jira Work Management forms, along with other reporting functions such as Dashboards, Filters, and JWM Reports. The chapter also covers how issues appear in each reporting feature and the factors that should be considered when deciding which to use.

Chapter 7, Managing Fields, Screens, and Issue Layouts, covers the basic function of custom fields, screens, and issue layouts, including how to add custom fields and the placement of the fields on screens. The chapter also covers custom field contexts and how to limit the display of fields on screens based on the combination of projects and issue types.

Chapter 8, Configuring Permissions and Simple Administration, covers the configuration of permissions based on the permission scheme and project roles for the Jira Work Management project. It will also cover how to add users to your project and associate them with Project Roles. Finally, the chapter covers simple administration available for project administrators and differentiates these abilities from the organization-level Jira Administrator role.

Chapter 9, Duplicating Projects and Starting Outside of the Box, covers how to create new projects based on the structure and shared schemes of existing projects. The chapter also gives some helpful guidance on considerations when creating projects and issues outside of the normal, simple creation process, including APIs and CSV imports. Finally, the chapter covers migrating existing Jira projects to Jira Work Management.

Chapter 10, Using Project Automation, covers the creation of automation rules, which are configurable by the Project Administrator. While Jira automation is very extensive and a large collection of rules are available, the chapter covers only the basic and most popular use cases for the tool.

To get the most out of this book

Getting started with the book is easy and little advanced preparation is needed. Start by creating a free Jira Cloud account – you can upgrade to a more fully functional version later, but the free subscription is good enough. Use your favorite internet browser and you will be good to go.

Requirement for the book
Jira Cloud subscription

> **Note**
> Familiarity with Jira will be helpful but is certainly not needed.

Download the color images

We also provide a PDF file that has color images of the screenshots and diagrams used in this book. You can download it here: `https://static.packt-cdn.com/downloads/9781803232003_ColorImages.pdf`.

Please note that this book uses a lot of screenshots of user interface for reference. You can find clearer images of these screenshots in the aforementioned URL.

Conventions used

There are a number of text conventions used throughout this book.

`Code in text`: Indicates code words in text, database table names, folder names, filenames, file extensions, pathnames, dummy URLs, user input, and Twitter handles. Here is an example: "Your code would resemble `Project = STAFF`."

Bold: Indicates a new term, an important word, or words that you see onscreen. For instance, words in menus or dialog boxes appear in **bold**. Here is an example: "You still have the option to change it at this point by clicking on the **Change template** button."

> **Tips or Important Notes**
> Appear like this.

Get in touch

Feedback from our readers is always welcome.

General feedback: If you have questions about any aspect of this book, email us at `customercare@packtpub.com` and mention the book title in the subject of your message.

Errata: Although we have taken every care to ensure the accuracy of our content, mistakes do happen. If you have found a mistake in this book, we would be grateful if you would report this to us. Please visit `www.packtpub.com/support/errata` and fill in the form.

Piracy: If you come across any illegal copies of our works in any form on the internet, we would be grateful if you would provide us with the location address or website name. Please contact us at `copyright@packt.com` with a link to the material.

If you are interested in becoming an author: If there is a topic that you have expertise in and you are interested in either writing or contributing to a book, please visit `authors.packtpub.com`.

Share Your Thoughts

Once you've read *Jira Work Management for Business Teams*, we'd love to hear your thoughts! Scan the QR code below to go straight to the Amazon review page for this book and share your feedback.

https://packt.link/r/1803232005

Your review is important to us and the tech community and will help us make sure we're delivering excellent quality content.

Section 1: Jira Work Management Basics

In this section, you will learn how Jira Work Management projects are different from other Jira projects and when they might best be used. You will also learn how to quickly create a project using a predefined template and add your first item of work.

This section contains the following chapters:

- *Chapter 1, Why Choose Jira Work Management?*
- *Chapter 2, Working with Project Templates*
- *Chapter 3, Creating Your First Project*

1

Why Choose Jira Work Management?

For years, Atlassian's flagship collection of products known as **Jira** has been a favorite for project and product managers. This also rings true for those working in the field of **information technology service management** (**ITSM**). Jira has come a long way since it debuted in 2002 as an issue- and bug-tracking tool, with several products now having been launched since the initial offering.

So, whether you are a seasoned veteran of the Jira world or brand new to this funny-sounding tool landscape, this book will be just what you need to get up and running with navigating the product known as **Jira Work Management** (**JWM**).

As these new Jira products have sprouted up, there has come additional functionality and, unfortunately to an extent, increased complexity in creating, using, and managing projects. Don't get me wrong—I love the flexibility and enhancements that have been made. But I also have years of experience working with the Jira toolset, and for new users and administrators, Jira can be daunting.

Having said all of that, it begs the question: *If many products are being offered by Atlassian, why should we choose JWM?* The quick answer is that JWM provides a simple and fast path to creating new projects in Jira while incorporating new and exciting functionality not found in other Jira-related products.

At its very essence, JWM is a retooling and rebranding of the initial **Jira Core** product for business projects. This chapter will describe the differences in the products to help ease the move into this next generation of the tool.

But just being the rebranding of an existing tool is not a good enough reason to choose to use JWM. So, what are some things that set it apart?

First, JWM integrates seamlessly with the existing Jira family of products such as **Jira Software (JSW)** and **Jira Service Management (JSM)** projects and the Jira Cloud platform **REpresentational State Transfer (REST) application programming interface (API)** functionality. This integration means there is already a familiarity with the general execution of Atlassian products and their great reputation.

Add to those reasons the powerful performance of built-in project automation, the simple process of project creation and setup, and a suite of new tools, and you have one of the best new project management products on the market.

In this chapter, we're going to cover the following main topics:

- Comparing project types in Jira
- Review of the Jira Core product
- What's new in JWM?
- New terms learned in this chapter

Upon completion of this chapter, you will be able to describe how JWM projects are different from other Jira projects and which situations are best suited to each product type.

Technical requirements

As JWM is only available in the Jira Cloud environment, the requirement for this chapter is simple: *access to a Jira Cloud environment.*

If you already have access to Jira Cloud, that's great—you're ready to go! If not, Atlassian provides a free JWM account for up to 10 users. You can create your account by going to `https://www.atlassian.com/try/cloud/signup?bundle=jira-core&edition=free` and following the instructions.

Comparing project types in Jira

Projects within Jira can be approached from two different viewpoints. One way is to treat a project as you would historically when thinking of projects. As noted by the **Project Management Institute (PMI)**:

"According to the PMBOK® Guide—Fourth edition (PMI, 2008a, p. 434), the definition of a project is a temporary endeavor undertaken to create a unique project service or result. Projects are temporary and close down on the completion of the work they were chartered to deliver." (Source: `https://bit.ly/3xoo0Ar`)

Another way to phrase the *temporary* nature of a project is to say that it has defined start and end dates. For example, think of building a house or a building or planning a wedding or a vacation. You know when you start to plan, and you know when the work or effort is finished.

This is certainly one way to approach a project in Jira, but the result will probably be dozens—or even hundreds—of projects in an organization's Jira instance. You will also have the added effort of closing down or archiving projects when completed.

However, I personally believe that most companies and organizations will view Jira projects as the ongoing work being performed by an internal team, whether that be a business team, a design team, or a product development team. While many organizations are often divided into **business units (BUs)**, those can easily be considered to be teams or might even be broken down into multiple teams or squads, depending on the size of the unit.

Projects within Jira fall into three closely related but distinct classes of products. These are **JWM**, **JSW**, and **JSM**. As acronyms help to shorten the text and bring focus to the intended objects, we will sprinkle these throughout the book.

While JSW and JSM projects are very robust and account for the majority of projects in most organizations, the old *Jira Core projects* (now JWM) have historically been seen as lesser cousins of the two more famous products. Thus, there was a need to bolster a somewhat dying brand within the toolset.

Rodney Nissen, also known as *The Jira Guy* (https://thejiraguy.com/) has cleverly captured this in a graphic, as shown here:

Figure 1.1 – The Jira Guy

No matter which type of project you intend to use, the creation of each begins with the same path. Start by simply clicking on the **Projects** menu option in the top navigation bar of Jira, followed by clicking on **Create project**, as illustrated in the following screenshot:

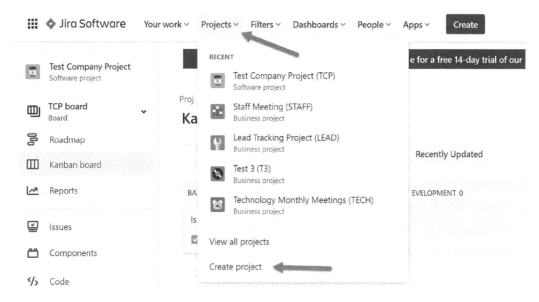

Figure 1.2 – Basic project creation

Each of the next subsections will give a brief overview of the three products, when those types of projects are best used, and—finally—a graphical representation of how to begin the creation process for each.

JWM projects

JWM projects are specifically referred to as *business projects* within Jira and are designed for typical organizational BUs such as **Human Resources** (**HR**), Finance, Legal, Marketing, Sales, Operations, Design, Shipping/Inventory, and Video production. While not all companies will have all these units, it speaks to the power and inclusiveness of JWM's ability to address these areas and perhaps more.

It is worthy of noting that JWM projects have some of the same shared underpinnings of JSW and JSM projects, thereby making it easy for projects of all types to communicate with each other. In fact, you are considered to be in a company-managed project when you create a JWM project. See the *Company-managed software projects* section for more on this.

Upon selecting **Create project**, the user is presented with an extensive list of JWM project templates. JWM project templates provide a quick means of getting your project set up by creating a base project, a defined workflow based on the template type, an accompanying board to match the workflow, and the various screens and permissions needed to administer the project. We will delve into JWM templates in more detail in the next chapter, but here is a small list to whet your appetite for what is coming and to give you a view of what the screen will look like when creating a project:

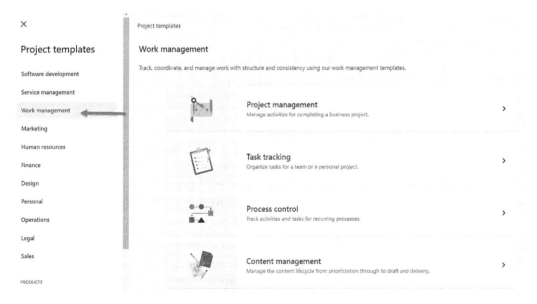

Figure 1.3 – JWM project templates

These business-type projects are more restrictive than JSW projects in that the board cannot be modified, and the columns on the JWM board, shown in the following screenshot, are actually controlled by the statuses found in the accompanying workflow:

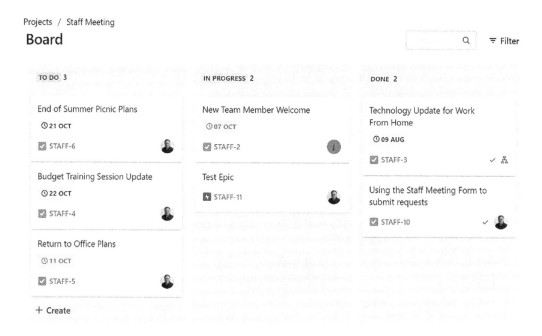

Figure 1.4 – JWM board

Next, let's take a look at the components and operation of JSW projects.

JSW projects

JSW projects, almost by definition, refer to projects primarily related to software development/engineering. These include typical workflows that transition through a combination of architectural design, development, code or peer review, merging of code, **quality assurance (QA)** testing, deployment, and possibly more. Or course, all these are flexible paths within JSW workflows.

Many organizations also utilize Jira's version of the agile world's favorite Scrum functionality. This includes releases, setting up Sprints, automatically moving uncompleted issues in a completed Sprint to the next Sprint, and so on. As you begin to create your JSW project, you will select from either a **Scrum**, **Kanban**, or **Bug Tracking** template.

The Jira Software Scrum template provides the user with pertinent information about the template type, along with the issue types included in the initial project setup and the statuses in the workflow. Since **Scrum** typically makes use of Sprints, the template workflow for that option will include simple statuses of **To Do**, **In Progress**, and **Done**.

The other primary type of JSW project is for **Kanban**. This agile framework is quickly catching on around the world, and Jira provides a mechanism to implement Kanban quickly.

While these types of projects gave rise to this product line of Jira, JSW projects have become the norm for all types of projects within organizations due to the many customizations available in the tool. But the complexity in the initial setup, maintenance, and administration for all that goes with these project types has now given rise to the need for a simpler option. In addition to providing simpler business-related projects via JWM, Atlassian has also introduced **team-managed projects**.

The **Bug Tracking** template enables the user to implement a project that not only tracks bugs but also connects issues back to improvements or new features that the bugs are associated with. All of these issue types, along with epics, tasks, and sub-tasks, can be seen on the same board and utilize the same workflow.

Team-managed software projects

Introduced as next-gen projects a few years ago, these software projects allow an independent team to fully administer and manage its projects without the need for a traditional Jira administrator. As with JWM projects, team-managed projects have a simpler interface but reduced functionality. In fact, much of the initial criticism of these projects is that they are too restrictive.

In response, Atlassian is continuing to add much-needed functionality to the tool while maintaining the independent administration that primarily separates it from all other types of projects in Jira. Teams can grant access to users on their own, create their own independent custom fields and automation, and manage their own workflows.

Company-managed software projects

Company-managed projects are the mainstay project types for most organizations using Jira. They provide the most functionality by utilizing shared custom fields, schemes for permissions, screens, workflows, issue types, notifications, and so on. All of these can be modified as necessary, although the user will need to be a Jira administrator to make changes to most of the objects.

Once you have chosen either Scrum or Kanban, you will then decide on **Team-managed** or **Company-managed** as the project type. As noted in the following screenshot, you will not be able to *convert* or change the type of a project once it is created. You will need to create a new project of the appropriate type and move any existing issues from the original project to the new project:

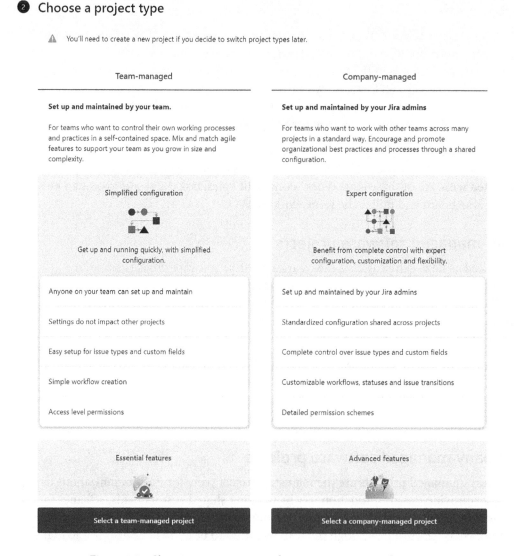

Figure 1.5 – Choosing a team-managed or company-managed project

JSM projects

JSM projects go back to more of the root of Jira's first offering of a *ticketing*-type tool. They are especially designed for receiving and processing helpdesk types of requests. Perhaps the favorite feature is the helpful **portal** function, which also incorporates easy-to-fill-in forms.

Another very useful functionality is the concept of non-licensed users (or customers) being able to submit requests. This is a customers feature where the user can be exterior to the organization or even anonymous. This saves on license fees for users who just need to submit a request.

However, for any user who needs to edit field values or transition issues, there is an added cost in that those who are handling the request must be added as *agents*, which requires an additional license fee.

Just as JWM has some built-in templates to get a project started, JSM also has a handful of templates available, as shown in the following screenshot:

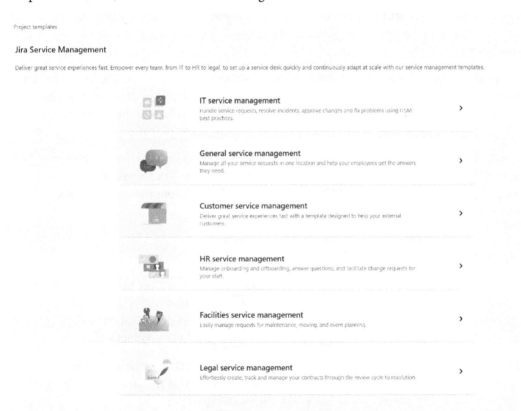

Figure 1.6 – JSM project templates

Now, let's take a quick look at how JWM differs from the old Jira Core product.

Review of the Jira Core product

In 2015, Atlassian split Jira into two different products—Jira Core and JSW. Jira Core was always billed as a simple way to get started with issue tracking and became the base product that was offered when new users came on board with the tool. The focus was on non-technical teams in an organization, oftentimes referred to as business teams.

JSW continues to be aimed at software development teams and provides the most functionality and flexibility of the two products. The two have lived side by side for nearly a decade in versions deployed on-premises (**Jira Server**) and in the cloud (**Jira Cloud**). **Data Center** versions are also available.

While Jira was always intended to be used by technical and non-technical teams alike, the introduction of the JSW product placed an emphasis on Agile development, release management, and software team-related reporting. In fact, the previous releases of Jira leading up to the JSW announcement had already begun implementing many of the features that were coming. As Jira continued to grow in capabilities, it also grew in complexity.

Perhaps the biggest knock against Jira by those newcomers dipping their toe into Atlassian waters for the first time was figuring out the beast that it had become. It seems that the namesake of *Gojira* (Japanese for Godzilla, and the inspiration for the shortened name of the tool) had to a certain extent become a monster for the rookie user.

To address this issue, Jira Core became the intended safe path into the waters. It kept many of the powerful functionality that had endeared it to the Jira fanbase but provided a simpler approach to getting started with the tool, and all without having to sacrifice what made Jira the best tool for the job for many people.

What's new in JWM?

After more than half a decade since the official rollout of the Jira Core branding, Atlassian decided that a makeover was due. In discussions with a selection of Jira users and Atlassian community leaders, Atlassian product managers and designers embarked on meeting the needs and desires of their customers in the Jira Core product makeover.

As already mentioned, while the underpinning of JWM projects has the same basic structure as company-managed software projects, it's the newest features that really set it apart from other Jira project types. Let's take a look at these here:

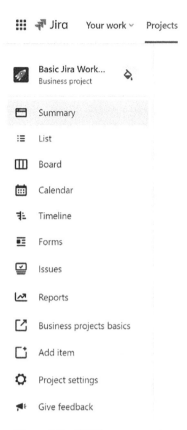

Figure 1.7 – JWM components

We will briefly look at the Jira board and new items here, but each will be expanded on in more detail in the chapters to come. These are listed as follows:

- **Summary**: This feature provides information through an activity stream for the project and statistics related to issue status, priorities, and assignees.

- **List**: This feature provides a list of issues for the project while displaying various fields (columns) for the particular issues. It also provides inline editing for each of the fields.

- **Board**: This is the standard board feature provided for most Jira projects, though it is limited and not editable for things such as the board filter or card and color displays.

- **Calendar**: This is an in-project calendar relating to issues within the project. It displays issues based on the due date and/or the start date.

- **Timeline**: This feature is similar to the **Roadmap** feature available for JSW projects. It displays issues in a Gantt format.

- **Forms**: Although listed in the plural form, there is actually just one form per project available at the time of writing this book. The form is simple to produce and uses an intake format, using drag and drop fields.

New terms learned in this chapter

Let's conclude the chapter by going through a list of new terms learned in this chapter, as follows:

- **JWM**: A rebranding of Jira Core Cloud and offered as a new product with many new features.

- **Jira Core**: An initial Atlassian base project management product closely aligned with business teams.

- **ITSM**: How IT teams deliver services to their customers and manage that delivery.

- **JSW**: Atlassian's project management tool aimed at software development teams.

- **JSM**: A rebranding of Jira Service Desk and Atlassian's ticket management system provided for helpdesk teams such as IT.

- **Project templates**: A set of preconfigured components and features used to quickly create new JWM projects.

- **Board**: A visualization of work as cards on a display made up of rows and columns.

- **Team-managed projects**: JSW projects that are self-contained and geared for individual team use. It is a rebranding of next-gen projects.

- **Company-managed projects**: JSW projects that use components that can be shared across multiple projects.

- **Jira Cloud**: Atlassian's platform for products based exclusively on access through the internet.

Summary

Well, there you have it—a concise yet thorough view into the origins of JWM and a discussion of where it fits in the Jira ecosystem.

In this chapter, you have learned about different project types in Jira and when to use them.

We also covered how the original Jira Core tool has changed from the initial offering to the new JWM product. Finally, we took a brief look at the new features available for JWM projects.

So, back to our original question: *Why choose JWM?* As you have seen, with the availability of multiple project templates and exciting new components such as an inline editable list, **Calendar**, **Forms**, and **Timeline**, it is the easiest and most complete product for business-related projects.

Utilizing this knowledge, you can now get started using Jira in the simplest manner available and be immediately successful in corralling that work into easy-to-use projects. You will be more organized than ever and have information at the tips of your fingers.

In the next chapter, we will learn all about the various JWM templates that are available and how the user can determine which one best fits their requirements.

2
Working with Project Templates

Over my years of working as a Jira administrator and Atlassian community leader, I have seen countless requests for and questions about creating projects based on **templates**. As you can imagine, there are many different mindsets as to what a *template* looks like for a project. Some want to create a custom template that satisfies the particular need they have, while others just want something quick and easy they can click on that will build the basic project objects needed.

Regardless of the motivation or exact need, the general concept that the user is looking for is a fast way to create a project that already has built-in schemes and objects—such as a board or list/queue—that mostly aligns with their basic requirement.

Historically, all of the Jira family of products—Jira Core (now **Jira Work Management**, or **JWM**), **Jira Software** (**JSW**), and Jira Service Desk (now **Jira Service Management**, or **JSM**)—have provided a single unique set of objects automatically created based on the tool used to create a project.

Although the user still cannot create their own custom *template*, it was—and still is—possible to create a project based on an existing project that will provide a commonly shared set of schemes and objects. We will explore the details of that in *Chapter 9, Duplicating Projects and Starting Outside of the Box*.

But in this chapter, we'll look at how JWM now brings a large set of preexisting templates (more than 20!) that allow the user to create a project based on a variety of functions, including major groups for the templates. This chapter will also explore the differences in each of the available templates and the underlying components, such as the workflow and board columns.

We are going to cover the following main topics in this chapter:

- What are JWM templates?
- How are JWM templates grouped?
- Exploring the information available for templates
- Deciding which template to use
- New terms learned in this chapter

Upon completion of this chapter, you will be able to describe the purpose and function of project templates for JWM projects and the groupings they roughly fall into. You will also be able to find and identify the various templates available. Templates will be your best way to create a new project, so knowing which templates are available and what they contain will be beneficial as you get started.

Technical requirements

As JWM is only available in the Jira Cloud environment, the requirement for this chapter is simple: *access to a Jira Cloud environment.*

If you already have access to Jira Cloud, that's great—you are ready to go! If not, Atlassian provides a free JWM account for up to 10 users. You can create your account by going to `https://www.atlassian.com/try/cloud/signup?bundle=jira-core&edition=free` and following the instructions.

What are JWM templates?

Project templates provide the user with a quick start for a project by automatically creating several technical components necessary to administer and use the project. We have already described in *Chapter 1, Why Choose Jira Work Management?,* how the process of creating a new project has the user pass through a phase of selecting a template to use. This is a necessary step as it establishes the workflow for cards on the project as well as columns that will appear on the board.

The steps in the workflow directly correlate to statuses for the project. Some common steps/statuses are **TO DO, IN PROGRESS, DONE**, and so on. Column names on the board will be the same as the status names. See the section entitled *How to read a workflow* later in this chapter for more on relationships between statuses.

Along with the board and workflow, other schemes will be automatically attached to the project for screens, permissions, and notifications. We will discuss how to administer and work with those objects in more detail in *Chapter 4, Modifying the Board, Workflow, and Associated Schemes*. Most of the project templates can be grouped or associated together along common themes or functions. We will explore that next.

How are JVM templates grouped?

There is not a hard and fast grouping of JWM templates. However, there were some themes in mind when the current list of templates was planned and built as the starter set for business projects.

Some of the templates will span multiple groupings or themes, such as those relating to task management and planning and content management. I will lump those into a group that I will simply call the **Basic Group**.

Again, templates might fall into multiple themes, but here is my take on groups, along with the templates that fall into each. This is only intended as a rough guide for the types of project templates that are available, but I think it is a beneficial guide to allow you to narrow your focus when selecting a new template.

Basic Group

These are common templates that many projects will use and are generic in terms of subject matter.

- **Content Management**: Manage the content life cycle from prioritization through to draft and delivery.

- **Task Tracking**: Organize tasks for a team or a personal project.

- **Personal Task Planner**: Stay organized and tackle your personal tasks easily.

Human Resources (HR)

These templates help with a variety to HR functions from prior to hiring to working with current employees.

- **Recruitment**: Monitor candidates and potential hires from application to offer.
- **New Employee Onboarding**: Track the progression of new hires, all the way from offer acceptance to day 1 on the job.
- **Performance Review**: Standardize your employees' performance evaluations and the peer-review process.

Finance

Financial projects can cover a wide range, including inventory or assets as well as reporting periods and budgeting.

- **Asset Creation**: Streamline the process of managing incoming asset creation requests.
- **Budget Creation**: Get everyone on the same page during the budget creation process.
- **Month-end Close**: Manage and simplify your month-end close process.
- **Procurement**: Standardize your procurement process and track all purchases from request to receipt.
- **RFP Process**: Roll out your **request for proposal** (**RFP**) process so that you can select the right vendor for the right job.

Legal

These templates have specialized workflows which assist in the normal process for legal file preparations.

- **Document Approval**: Manage documents from creation to approval.
- **IP Infringement**: Handle claims efficiently and quickly for **intellectual property** (**IP**) infringement.
- **Policy Management**: Track the moving parts involved in managing policies and procedures.

Marketing/Sales

Marketing and sales type projects tend to follow some common campaign processes or journeys. These templates will be especially helpful in that area due to how the workflows are organized.

- **Campaign Management**: Drive a marketing campaign from idea to execution.

- **Email Campaign**: Plan and execute email campaigns.

- **Go-to-Market**: Coordinate a **go-to-market** (**GTM**) launch for your product or business.

- **Lead Tracking**: Track sales leads from opportunity through to close.

- **Sales Pipeline**: Manage your sales pipeline from lead to converted customer, all in one place.

- **Web Design Process**: For designers and developers to track web design tasks and stay aligned.

Operations

Most organizations are going to have need for simple project and task related processes. This grouping provides clear focus on getting events and tasks done.

- **Project Management**: Manage activities for completing a business project.

- **Process Control**: Track activities and tasks for recurring processes.

- **Event Planning**: Empower teams in their planning for the next event, big or small.

Next, we will delve into the details of each template and cover some basics of how to read a workflow.

Exploring the information available for templates

In the previous section, we listed the standard set of project templates that come *out of the box* with JWM. However, in the subsections to come, there will be more details provided for each template. These details will include general explanations of why each template is provided, along with the **issue types** and **workflow** connected to the template.

The intention is for the text to help guide you as to when each template might best be used. The issue types will provide some clarity as to the type of work best suited for the templates and the statuses or steps in the workflow that will be aligned with the project.

It should be noted that the pages to follow will be mostly screenshots of the current JWM templates at the time of writing this book. As Atlassian has gone to a concerted effort to create, configure and detail the templates, it is a good idea to let the tool speak for itself for those descriptions. Keep in mind that the current templates available in the product might be somewhat different in comparison to what is provided here.

Issue types, workflow, and board relationships

These are some of the most basic, yet powerful parts of JSW and JWM projects, but how they are configured in the two tools also provides some of the largest differences in the tools. We will not belabor the point too much by detailing the workings of JSW projects here, but we will note the relations of these major components for JWM.

Historically, it is the board that provides the most vivid visualization of the work being done on a project or by a team. Whether it be a Kanban or a Sprint board, it is undeniably powerful to see the cards and their progress on the board.

Simply put, boards are made up of horizontal rows called *swimlanes* and vertical columns that represent the activities performed on the project, such as design, development, or testing. In JWM projects, these columns will be a one-to-one match with the statuses in the project workflow.

Currently, JWM projects do not allow multiple workflows to be associated with a board. Therefore, while there might be multiple issue types associated with the project, all issue types must be associated with one and only one workflow. We will go into more depth about configuring and modifying components in *Chapter 4, Modifying the Board, Workflow, and Associated Schemes.*

How to read a workflow

As we will be showing many details about each template, including workflow images, this seems like a good time to discuss how to read a workflow. At a quick glance, we see that workflows are made up of **statuses** (think steps) and **transitions** (think paths). The workflows that follow help guide the user by providing named transitions from one status to the next. See *Figure 2.1* and *Figure 2.2* as visual references to our discussion here.

Statuses appear as different colored boxes, while transitions are lines connecting the statuses or identifying the path from one status to another. *Figure 2.1* and *Figure 2.2* have the names of the transitions turned on so that it is easier to tell the direction of the flow as well as describe the action taking place. It is always good to name transitions using a verb when possible.

The workflow begins with a gray circle and a **Create** transition. Note that cards might flow in either direction. The placement of the words on the transition denotes the direction of the flow—so, in this example, when an issue is created, it will land in the **TO DO** status. From there, the issue can only move forward to the **IN PROGRESS** status using a **Start Progress** transition.

Once an issue is in progress, it can either travel forward to the **DONE** status using a **Done** transition or return to the **TO DO** status via a **Stop Progress** transition. Finally, from the **DONE** status, an issue might be reopened and return to the **TO DO** status for a **Reopen** transition, or it might return to the **IN PROGRESS** status by using a **Reopen and start progress** transition.

Notice in the following screenshot that all statuses fall into one of three categories—**TO DO** (the box under the **Create** transition heading), **IN PROGRESS** (far-right box), or **DONE** (bottom box). In this case, it just so happens that the status names also match with the status category names:

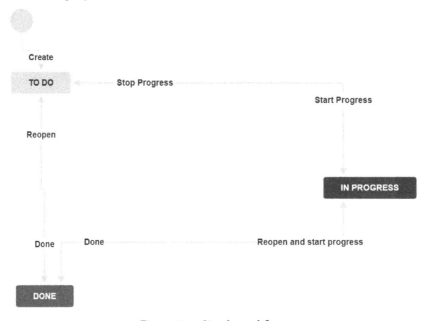

Figure 2.1 – Simple workflow

It should be noted that a status may have a single **All** transition attached to it, as in the following screenshot. This simply means that the flow of a card can go from any other status in the workflow to that status. Otherwise, cards must move in a linear fashion from one step to the next, as in *Figure 2.2*:

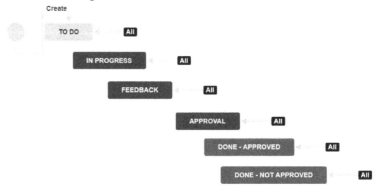

Figure 2.2 – Workflow utilizing All transitions

Now that we have some basics on how to read templates, let's delve into some details.

Project Management

This first template is perhaps the most used template for JWM projects and is a great template to use to create your first business project. The name is generic on purpose and covers a wide range of instances where the template can be used. You can see a representation of this template here:

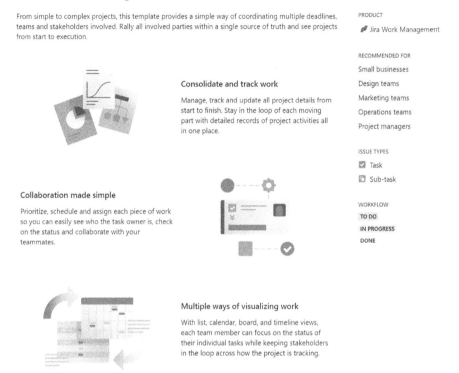

Figure 2.3 – Project Management template

The **Project Management** template is the same as we used as the example in *Figure 2.1*. It is very simple in nature and provides an easy start to using JWM projects. The workflow is represented here:

Figure 2.4 – Project Management workflow

Task Tracking

The simplest of the initial set of project templates, the **Task Tracking** template is all about providing a quick way of implementing a traditional to-do list. The twist is that you can use a two-tiered approach with both **Task** and **Sub-task** issue types, as illustrated in the following screenshot:

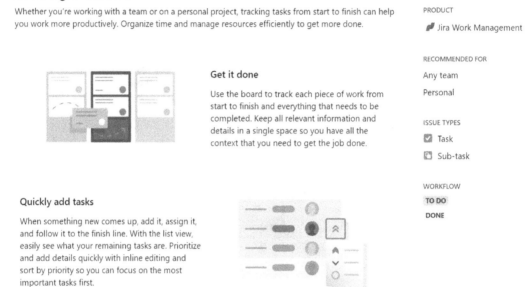

Whether you're working with a team or on a personal project, tracking tasks from start to finish can help you work more productively. Organize time and manage resources efficiently to get more done.

PRODUCT

Jira Work Management

RECOMMENDED FOR

Any team

Personal

ISSUE TYPES

Task

Sub-task

WORKFLOW

TO DO

DONE

Get it done

Use the board to track each piece of work from start to finish and everything that needs to be completed. Keep all relevant information and details in a single space so you have all the context that you need to get the job done.

Quickly add tasks

When something new comes up, add it, assign it, and follow it to the finish line. With the list view, easily see what your remaining tasks are. Prioritize and add details quickly with inline editing and sort by priority so you can focus on the most important tasks first.

Figure 2.5 – Task Tracking template

This is a very straightforward workflow that goes from **TO DO** to **DONE**, as illustrated in the following screenshot. It can be reopened if necessary:

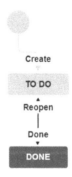

Figure 2.6 – Task Tracking workflow

Content Management

Today's world is awash with content. Between blogs and websites and postings of every kind, we need some help with managing the creation of all that information. The **Content Management** template provides a single issue type of **Asset** with a simple but efficient workflow, as illustrated in the following screenshot:

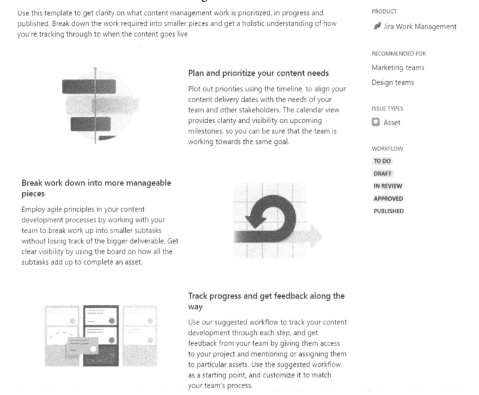

Figure 2.7 – Content Management template

The workflow provides a path for creating a draft, having it reviewed and then approved, and finally sending it off to the world by publishing it. There is flexibility provided in the review and draft stages to allow for any needed revisions, as illustrated in the following screenshot:

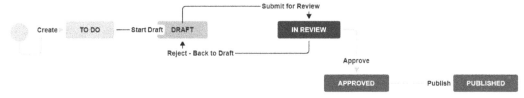

Figure 2.8 – Content Management workflow

Document Approval

Very similar to the **Content Management** template is the **Document Approval** template. Again, with the amount of information being produced in the current age, there continues to be a growing need for processes related to documents and content. You can see a representation of this template in the following screenshot:

Figure 2.9 – Document Approval template

The workflow is also very linear in following a path of creating a draft, having it reviewed (in this case, possibly reviewed twice), and then getting it approved, as illustrated in the following screenshot:

Figure 2.10 – Document Approval workflow

Web Design Process

The **Web Design Process** template follows more of an ideation thought process, where an idea is formulated, a design is created, and the resulting wireframes or sketches are tested. Finally, the product is launched after all the steps have been reviewed and agreed upon. You can see a representation of this template in the following screenshot:

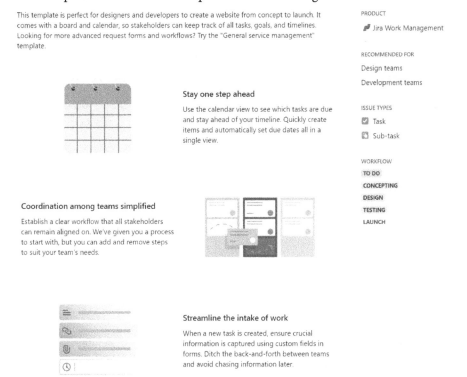

Figure 2.11 – Web Design Process template

The workflow has a classic **All** transitions concept whereby cards can flow easily back and forth between each step, allowing for maximum collaboration, as illustrated in the following screenshot:

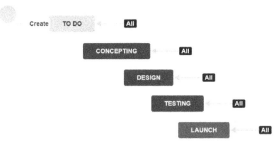

Figure 2.12 – Web Design Process workflow

Recruitment

Employees seem to be on the move more than ever now, with working-from-home schemes and migrations of positions across states, provinces, and even country borders. The **Recruitment** template, as illustrated in the following screenshot, provides for the process of receiving candidates and tracking them through the hiring process:

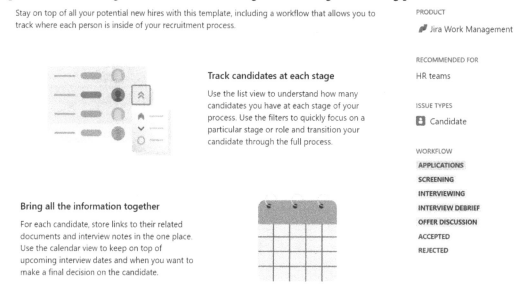

Stay on top of all your potential new hires with this template, including a workflow that allows you to track where each person is inside of your recruitment process.

Track candidates at each stage

Use the list view to understand how many candidates you have at each stage of your process. Use the filters to quickly focus on a particular stage or role and transition your candidate through the full process.

Bring all the information together

For each candidate, store links to their related documents and interview notes in the one place. Use the calendar view to keep on top of upcoming interview dates and when you want to make a final decision on the candidate.

PRODUCT

🖋 Jira Work Management

RECOMMENDED FOR

HR teams

ISSUE TYPES

🗂 Candidate

WORKFLOW

APPLICATIONS
SCREENING
INTERVIEWING
INTERVIEW DEBRIEF
OFFER DISCUSSION
ACCEPTED
REJECTED

Figure 2.13 – Recruitment template

The workflow for recruiting is more linear in nature, with off-ramps available at a variety of points to reject any candidates not syncing with the position. Interviews are done, debriefs and discussions happen, and the final outcome of the candidate is decided upon, as illustrated in the following screenshot:

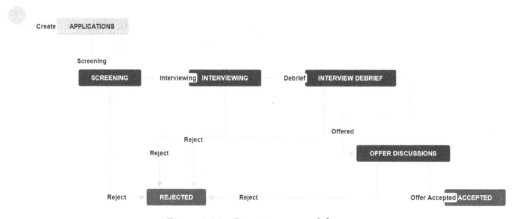

Figure 2.14 – Recruitment workflow

New Employee Onboarding

After your successful use of the Recruitment project, it is time to onboard your new employee! Get your employees started off right by collecting and reviewing pertinent documents, setting up computers and **information technology** (**IT**) equipment, and then be ready to welcome them on their first day. You can see a representation of the **New Employee Onboarding** template in the following screenshot:

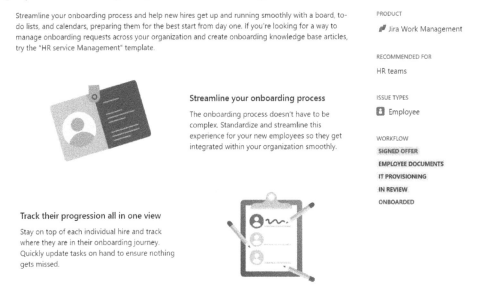

Figure 2.15 – New Employee Onboarding template

The workflow is fairly simple and provides for much flexibility as each of the statuses uses the **All** transition, as illustrated in the following screenshot:

Figure 2.16 – New Employee Onboarding workflow

Performance Review

Now that those new employees are onboarded and at work, you will eventually need to carry out a **performance review** on each person. This template provides easy tracking of these reviews by utilizing issue types for the employee, tasks, and sub-tasks. The combination provides for full coverage and is illustrated in the following screenshot:

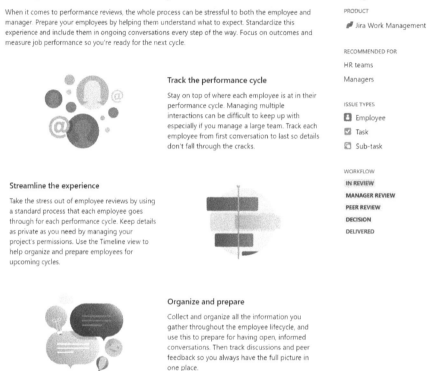

Figure 2.17 – Performance Review template

The workflow provides for different levels of review, culminating in a decision that can then be shared with the employee, as illustrated in the following screenshot:

Figure 2.18 – Performance Review workflow

Lead Tracking

As the name implies, the **Lead Tracking** template utilizes the **Lead** issue type to follow sales opportunities through the sales cycle. Sales pipelines are the lifeblood of revenue-producing streams, and losing track of opportunities or allowing them to stall unnoticed can have significant impacts on a company. You can see a representation of this template in the following screenshot:

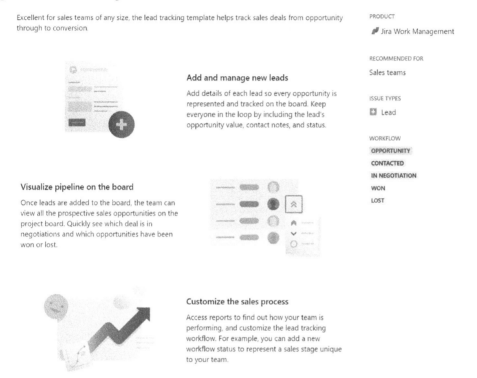

Excellent for sales teams of any size, the lead tracking template helps track sales deals from opportunity through to conversion.

Add and manage new leads

Add details of each lead so every opportunity is represented and tracked on the board. Keep everyone in the loop by including the lead's opportunity value, contact notes, and status.

Visualize pipeline on the board

Once leads are added to the board, the team can view all the prospective sales opportunities on the project board. Quickly see which deal is in negotiations and which opportunities have been won or lost.

Customize the sales process

Access reports to find out how your team is performing, and customize the lead tracking workflow. For example, you can add a new workflow status to represent a sales stage unique to your team.

PRODUCT

Jira Work Management

RECOMMENDED FOR

Sales teams

ISSUE TYPES

Lead

WORKFLOW

OPPORTUNITY

CONTACTED

IN NEGOTIATION

WON

LOST

Figure 2.19 – Lead Tracking template

Use the workflow to record the wins and losses experienced in your pipeline while tracking through initial contacts, negotiations, and the final outcome, as illustrated in the following screenshot:

Figure 2.20 – Lead Tracking workflow

Procurement

The **Procurement** template helps to ensure that your project keeps track of your purchase orders as well as recurring needs from year to year. Use due dates to guide your priorities and note the details of orders. You can see a representation of this template in the following screenshot:

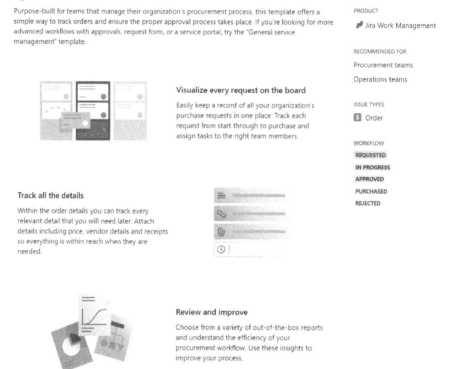

Purpose-built for teams that manage their organization's procurement process, this template offers a simple way to track orders and ensure the proper approval process takes place. If you're looking for more advanced workflows with approvals, request form, or a service portal, try the "General service management" template.

PRODUCT

Jira Work Management

RECOMMENDED FOR

Procurement teams

Operations teams

Visualize every request on the board

Easily keep a record of all your organization's purchase requests in one place. Track each request from start through to purchase and assign tasks to the right team members.

ISSUE TYPES

Order

WORKFLOW

REQUESTED
IN PROGRESS
APPROVED
PURCHASED
REJECTED

Track all the details

Within the order details you can track every relevant detail that you will need later. Attach details including price, vendor details and receipts so everything is within reach when they are needed.

Review and improve

Choose from a variety of out-of-the-box reports and understand the efficiency of your procurement workflow. Use these insights to improve your process.

Figure 2.21 – Procurement template

The workflow provides for approvals of orders following the initial request and reviews. It is mostly linear in nature, while reviews lead to a final outcome. You can see an illustration of the workflow here:

Figure 2.22 – Procurement workflow

Sales Pipeline

One philosophy of sales is the more contacts and opportunities, the better. Another is to focus on solid leads produced by well-thought-out campaigns for a higher percentage of conversions. Either way, a **sales pipeline** is crucial to support both. Track your customers with this template, from first contact to the close. You can see a representation of the **Sales Pipeline** template in the following screenshot:

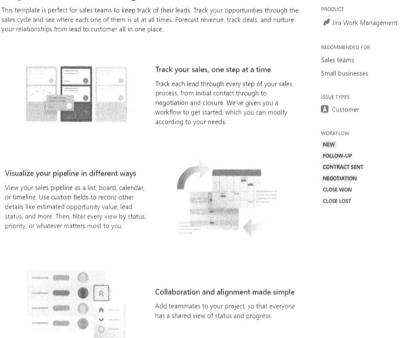

Figure 2.23 – Sales Pipeline template

Sales pipelines tend to have more of a linear workflow, but this one allows for flexibility in the path as well. With **Won** and **Lost** statuses, it will also be easy to report on the results of opportunities. You can see an illustration of the workflow here:

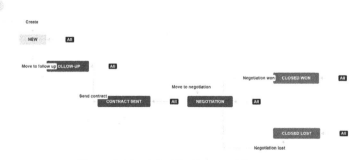

Figure 2.24 – Sales Pipeline workflow

Email Campaign

Let's face it—email is NOT dead! **Email campaigns** are still an effective way to reach customers and communicate sales, product offerings, company news, and more. This template incorporates **Asset**, **Task**, and **Sub-task** issue types to help track emails themselves and the efforts needed to produce them. You can see a representation of the **Email Campaign** template in the following screenshot:

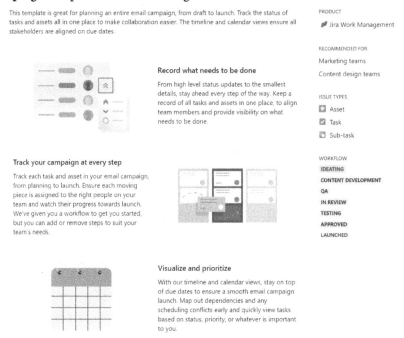

Figure 2.25 – Email Campaign template

There are several types of email campaigns that an organization can use, so this workflow provides the flexibility to skip columns when needed or proceed in a linear path, as illustrated in the following screenshot:

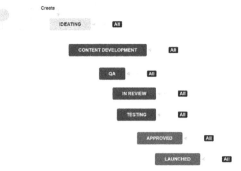

Figure 2.26 – Email Campaign workflow

Budget Creation

Few people like to create a budget, but they are very necessary to help control your finances. The **Budget Creation** template helps to pass a budget along for feedback, reviews, and approvals. At the end of the process, you can track approvals. You can see a representation of this template in the following screenshot:

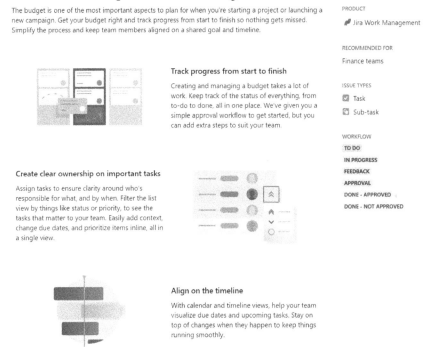

Figure 2.27 – Budget Creation template

Some budgets are more involved than others and need to pass through each step of the workflow. Others can skip columns that do not apply with these flexible steps of the **All** transitions, as illustrated in the following screenshot:

Figure 2.28 – Budget Creation workflow

Personal Task Planner

There is a myriad of **personal task planners** available to us. They appear in many different styles and formats. But why not just have Jira help you with what it does best—tracking tasks! Even at a personal level, a project built from the personal task planner will integrate well with other projects in your instance and provide a single place to see all of your work. You can see a representation of the **Personal Task Planner** template in the following screenshot:

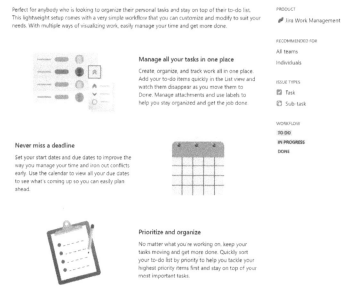

Figure 2.29 – Personal Task Planner template

The workflow cannot get much simpler than this—the classic **TO DO**, **IN PROGRESS**, **DONE** format that involves just one status of each category. Issues will be placed in the **TO DO** status when created and then moved to **IN PROGRESS** when started. Finally, the issue is simply moved to **DONE** when completed. You can see an illustration of the workflow in the following screenshot:

Figure 2.30 – Personal Task Planner workflow

Wow, that's a lot of templates! And it doesn't even show all of the current ones that exist for you to use. Next, let's take a look at some guidance for which template to use.

Deciding which template to use

With the outstanding list of built-in templates to use for JWM projects, which one should you use? Of course, the first clue is to ask yourself: *What am I trying to accomplish?* And the next logical step is to take a look at the descriptions of each project template found in the previous pages of this chapter or peruse the online descriptions within the tool itself.

Pay close attention to the issue types used by the templates along with the actual workflow implemented behind the scenes for the project. As we mentioned in the *Issue types, workflow, and board relationships* section, only a single workflow will be available for all issue types in the project. Remember that the statuses in the workflow will relate to the columns that are displayed on the board.

Do not get too hung up on the order of the statuses in the workflow as you will be able to rearrange the columns of the board after everything has been created. We will discuss that more in *Chapter 4*, *Modifying the Board, Workflow, and Associated Schemes*.

New terms learned in this chapter

Let's conclude the chapter by going through a list of new terms learned in this chapter, as follows:

- **Project templates**: A set of preconfigured components and features used to quickly create new JWM projects.
- **Issue type**: The identification of the type of work being done. This field is required for all new issues.
- **Workflow**: The path that work progresses through from start to finish, moving from step to step from **CREATE** to **DONE**.
- **Statuses**: The recognized name for steps in a workflow.
- **Transitions**: The paths from status to status in a workflow.

Summary

As mentioned earlier, JWM is different from the other Jira products partly because there are several pre-built project templates available to get you started quickly. We have explored the rough groupings of the templates, and then we did an in-depth dive into each template to explore the issue types and workflows each one uses.

Now that you have this knowledge, you know that the fastest way to create a project is by using a template, and you can now quickly identify which template to use based on the details provided by the template.

In the next chapter, we will build upon the templates just discussed by creating our first project. Once that is accomplished, we will explore what is available.

3
Creating Your First Project

Now that we have a lot of the preliminaries out of the way, let's get down to some real work. As you might have already guessed, the first step will be to create a project. We will walk through an example using the project management template, as it is the one that is most widely used.

This will begin our hands-on experience with the tool and we will follow the same process, in terms of how objects are created, as we progress from chapter to chapter. We will follow that up by creating our first issues and discovering how they are displayed on the board. Then, we will take a look at some of the administrative aspects of the tool that are automatically created when you build a project.

In this chapter, we are going to cover the following main topics:

- The process of creating a new project
- What's next after creating a project?
- The administration components of Jira Work Management projects

By the end of this chapter, you will have created your first Jira Work Management project and seen some initial issues. Additionally, you will be able to interact with the various administrative functions that are associated with the project.

Technical requirements

As Jira Work Management is only available in the Jira Cloud environment, the requirement for this chapter is simple: *access to a Jira Cloud environment.*

If you already have access to Jira Cloud, that is great – you are ready to go! If not, Atlassian provides a free Jira Work Management account for up to 10 users. You can create your account by navigating to `https://www.atlassian.com/try/cloud/signup?bundle=jira-core&edition=free` and following the instructions.

Let's create a project!

We will begin by selecting the **Projects** option in the top navigation bar and then selecting **Create project**:

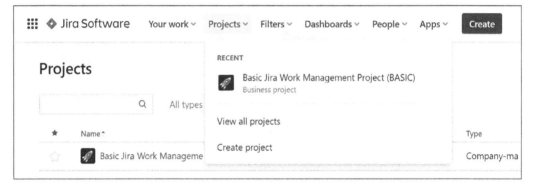

Figure 3.1 – The creating a project menu option

As previously discussed in *Chapter 2, Working with Project Templates*, there will immediately be a list of project templates displayed for Jira Work Management. At the time of writing, there are approximately 20 templates available. *Figure 3.2* shows just a subset of what is available:

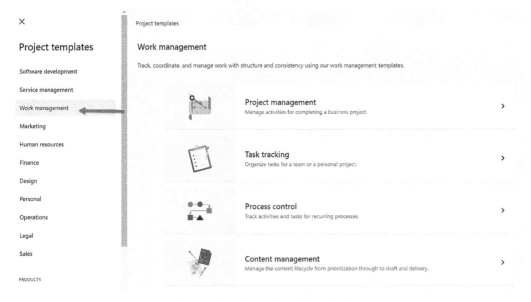

Figure 3.2 – Project template selection

For our first project, we will click on the first option, that is, **Project management**. Next, we will view the template details for our selection:

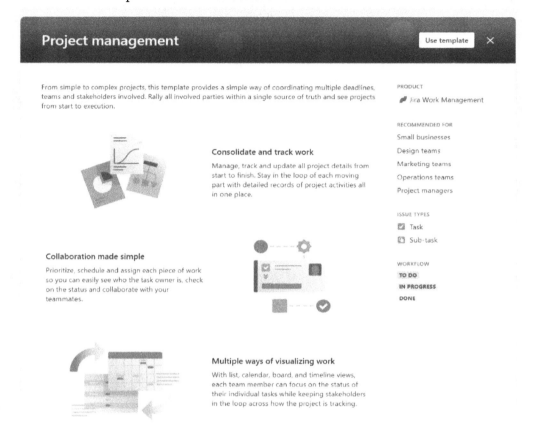

Figure 3.3 – Project management template details

There is a lot of information available on this details page, including the issue types used by the project and the steps in the workflow. Additionally, there are some general descriptions regarding how the template applies to the work you are doing, the components that will be available for the project (such as a list, calendar, or board), and how it aids with collaboration. This is intended to be more of a guide to ensure it is the right project template that you wish to create.

After your review, simply click on the **Use template** button. That will bring you to *Figure 3.4*, where you will give your project a name:

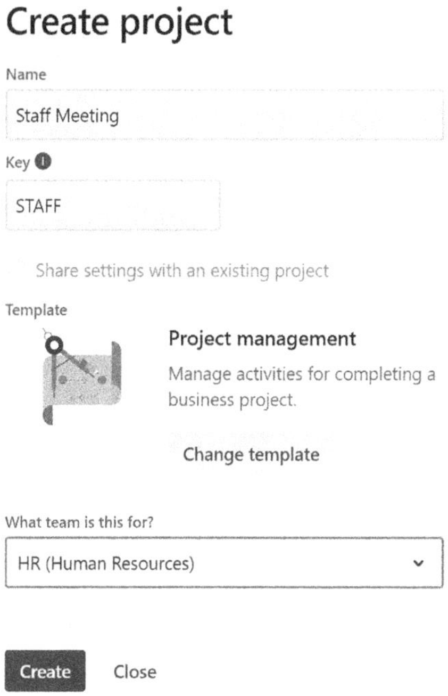

Create project

Name

Staff Meeting

Key ⓘ

STAFF

Share settings with an existing project

Template

Project management

Manage activities for completing a business project.

Change template

What team is this for?

HR (Human Resources) ⌄

Create   Close

Figure 3.4 – Naming the project

Initially, when this window is displayed, each of the fields will be empty. I have added some text as an example of the type of information that can be entered. Here's a rundown of each field:

- **Name**: The name of the project is your choosing. This value can easily be updated at any time if you change your mind. You should not spend too much time trying to create the perfect name right now – your priority is to get the project created. For our test project, I have chosen to create one based on recurring company staff meeting presentations.

- **Key**: The key is a short descriptor for the project and will probably be the most known part of an issue's ID. The key is required to be at least two characters in length, no more than 10 characters, and must start with a letter. All values for the key will be in uppercase by default, so do take that into consideration when creating the value. Changing the value of the key after it has been created can cause potential disconnects or other problems, so be careful when assigning.

- **Template**: This is just a final check that this is the template you want to use. You still have the option to change it at this point by clicking on the **Change template** button.

- **What team is this for?**: This is used by the internal Atlassian Jira Work Management product team to get a good feel for the types of teams using JWM projects. You will not be able to use the value in any other place in Jira. This field is optional.

For your first project, feel free to use whatever name and key you would like.

> **Important Note**
>
> Only project administrators or Jira administrators will be able to create new projects if you are not also subscribed to Jira Software or Jira Service Management. If you have either of those in addition to JWM, you must be a Jira administrator to create a project.
>
> Additionally, the project key will not be reusable for other projects in the future unless the entire original project using that key has been deleted.

Finally, click on the **Create** button to finish the new setup of your project. That's it! Your first project has been created! Let's take a closer look at what it produces.

The project board

When the project creation process is complete, you most likely will be directed to the project board. Notice, in the menu on the left-hand side, that you can easily navigate back to the board at any time by clicking on the **Board** option.

The board will initially be created with columns that match the statuses of the workflow. Please refer back to the project template details in *Figure 3.3*, which shows the statuses that have been created in the workflow – in this case, **TO DO**, **IN PROGRESS**, and **DONE**.

We will go into more depth about how the board operates and how to make changes in *Chapter 4, Modifying the Board, Workflow, and Associated Schemes*:

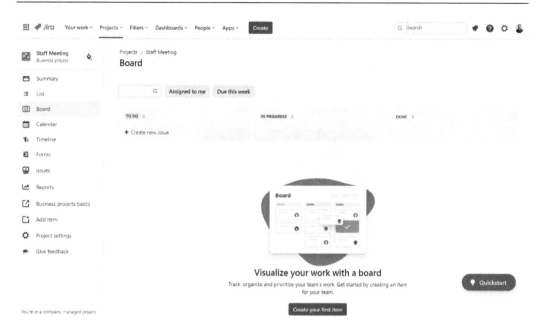

Figure 3.5 – The project board

We have explored the basics of project creation and gotten familiar with some of the tools. Where do we go from here?

The project has been created – now what?

Now that the project has processed and created the initial toolset based on the template used, what should our next steps be? While still on the board, there is a button available with a light bulb icon and the word **Quickstart**. Let's explore it by clicking on the button.

Doing so will display a popup on the right-hand side, as shown in *Figure 3.6*. The purpose of the quickstart window is to offer more information and guidance about each of the components available with a Jira Work Management project. As you explore each of these components, they will be checked off to give you visibility as to which items you have reviewed.

The downward-pointing caret will open additional information about the component. You can then click on the **Guide me** button to receive more in-depth information about the tool. We will explore each component, in additional detail, in *Chapters 5, JWM Toolset – Summary, Lists, Timelines, and the Calendar*, and *Chapter 6, Forms, Dashboards, and Reports*. To collapse the detailed information, just click on the upward-pointing arrow for that section:

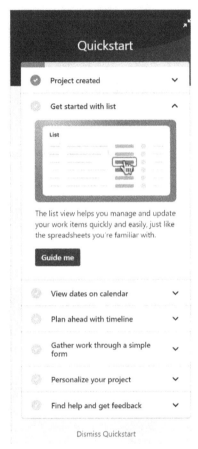

Figure 3.6 – Quickstart

The quickstart button will be available on the board until you click on the **Dismiss Quickstart** option at the bottom of the popup. If you simply want to close the popup for the time being but still have it available, click on the two arrows to minimize the window in the upper-right corner of the popup. However, even when you have dismissed the quickstart option, you can still get it back. Simply click on your avatar in the upper-right corner of the top navigation bar and select **Open Quickstart**.

In the next few sections, we will explore the various ways in which to create an issue/work item and see how it is displayed on the board.

Creating your first issue

There are at least three different places where you can begin creating your first issue. This is also a good time to discuss some terminology. Within the Jira product family, the term used to represent a piece of work to be done is **Issue**.

However, note that there are other words that you will come across that carry out the same work. In *Figure 3.5*, you can see the word **Item** in the bottom-center box. Once the issue/item has been created and appears on the board, it is often referred to as a **Card**. Regardless of which term is used, please understand that they all refer to the same piece of work. However, for clarity, we will refer to it as an issue, as the standard term for the remainder of this book.

Additionally, just as you can refer to the work in different ways, there is no one preferred method to create an issue. We will walk through each option as follows: options 1 and 2 are the most basic, while option 3 provides the opportunity to enter the most information. Later, in *Chapter 6, Forms, Issues, Dashboards, and Reports*, we will learn how to use forms to create an issue.

Creating option 1

Let's begin with the first creation method. As observed under the **Visualize your work with a board** section in *Figure 3.5*, there is a button at the bottom of the screen for **Create your first item**. When you click on that button, you will see something similar to *Figure 3.7*:

Figure 3.7 – Creating an issue

Clicking on the button will open a textbox in the first column on the board and will display a **Start typing…** phrase. It is really that simple – you just type a very short description of the work to be done and click on the **Save** button:

Figure 3.8 – Issue creation directly on board

Now let's look at another function to create issues.

Creating option 2

Alternatively, you can create a new item of work by clicking on the + **Create new issue** button at the bottom of the first column (**TO DO**) on the board. This will display the same view as shown in *Figure 3.5*, where you can begin typing the name of your first issue. Both options will bring you to the same spot on the card.

Creating option 3

Finally, you can create an issue by clicking on the **Create** button in the top navigation bar:

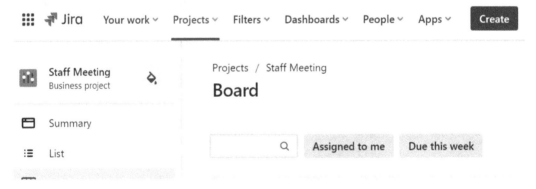

Figure 3.9 – Create an issue via the top navigation bar

Clicking on the **Create** button will display the **issue Create** screen for this project. As we discovered in the first two options for creating a new issue, the user is only able to type in the name of the issue. Informally, this is also known as the card title or issue name. However, more formally, it is referred to, in Jira, as the **Summary**.

Options 1 and 2 are intended to be very quick methods of creating a new issue or card. The issue will use the default issue type for the project (that is, the issue type at the top of the list of issue types in the issue type scheme. Please refer to *Chapter 8, Configuring Permissions and Simple Administration*, for details regarding how to change the default issue type).

As you can see, in *Figure 3.10*, using the **Create** button in the top navigation bar will provide the user with the most flexibility when creating a new issue. One advantage to this option is that you can use a different issue type other than the default. Another advantage is that you can insert information into additional fields at the same time you create the issue. Please refer to *Chapter 7, Managing Fields, Screens, and Issue Layouts*, for more information on how to control the fields used by the **Create** screen:

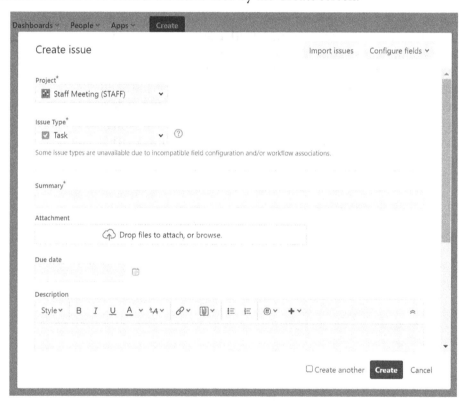

Figure 3.10 – Creating a screen

This is a great time to add values for fields such as the due date, priority, description, and more. The **Due date** field will appear in the card view on the board (as shown in *Figure 3.12*) as well as be visible in the calendar view. The start date will be used to properly visualize the work on the timeline view.

Of course, you can always update the details of the card later, even if you are using one of the quick methods for creating a new issue.

Back to the board

With Jira Software projects, the board is the primary way for users to interact with the issues that have been created. While Jira Work Management gives you new components to view and work with issues, the board remains a key visual method for viewing your work.

Let's take a look at some functions of the board. To move a card to the next step in the workflow (for instance, to the next column or any other available column), simply click on the card and drag it to the desired available column.

As you can see in the following screenshot, the card can go to two different columns – either the **IN PROGRESS** column or the **DONE** column, as noted by the columns being highlighted with different colors. It is confusing sometimes as to which status the card will settle into when released, particularly if the card is straddling both columns. All the available columns/statuses will be highlighted in a light shade of blue (as indicated by the **DONE** column in the following screenshot). However, one column/status will be highlighted a light shade of green. When the mouse is released, the card will fall into the status with the light green color (as indicated by the **IN PROGRESS** column in the following screenshot):

Figure 3.11 – Moving a card

Additional information will also be displayed on the card while on the board if those fields are populated. By default, the **Due date** option will appear on the card. You can view this in *Figure 3.12* represented by the January dates. If the field has not been populated, there will simply be no value displayed – as shown in the card in *Figure 3.11*.

Also, by default, the card will be assigned to the user who pulls the card into a new status or column. In the following example, we see that no cards are assigned in the first column (**TO DO**). However, we see an avatar for the user assigned to the cards in both the middle and last columns. If the user does not have an avatar linked to their profile, or for security reasons is not making their image available, the user's initials will be displayed:

Figure 3.12 – Multiple cards on a board

We have now created issues/cards and seen how they appear on boards. At this point we can create and use projects to accomplish our work. Next, let's look at how we can tweak the administration to get more flexibility and function.

Accessing the Jira Work Management Administration components

Although we will go into the administration details more fully *Chapter 7, Managing Fields, Screens, and Issue Layouts*, and *Chapter 8, Configuring Permissions and Simple Administration*, at this point, it is helpful to be able to find simple administration information. However, to do that, you need to know where to look and what to look for.

To gain access to administrative tools and information, you must be a project administrator. This means that the user must have an administrator project role and that role should be linked to the administer projects permission in the permission scheme attached to the project. We will discuss this in more detail in *Chapter 8, Configuring Permissions and Simple Administration*. As a side note, just because the user is a Jira administrator or *system* administrator, that does not automatically give the user access to administer projects.

Click on the **Project settings** option on the left-hand side menu to enter the project administration area. If you do not see the **Project settings** option, then you do not have project administrator permissions:

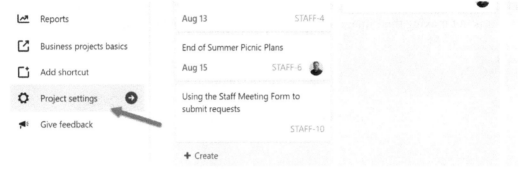

Figure 3.13 – Project settings

Project details

Selecting **Project settings** will advance you to the project details window, as shown in *Figure 3.15*. This is where you can change a variety of settings for the project:

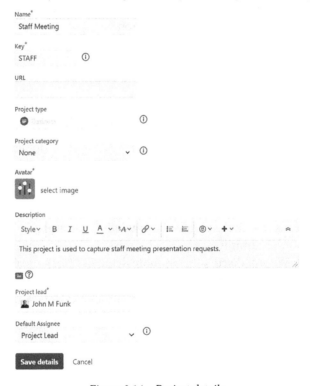

Figure 3.14 – Project details

The following options are available:

- **Name**: This is the location where you can change the name of the project that was populated during the project creation process. You can change the name at any time. It is a required field.

- **Key**: As with the name, this is where the key can be changed. Again, you should use caution when changing it. It is a required field.

- **URL**: This provides a link to a user-provided external site that contains more details about the project.

- **Project Type**: This is used to set to a value of **Business** for Jira Work Management projects and cannot be changed.

- **Project Category**: This field will be blank for your first project as no project categories exist. You need to click on the information icon to create your first category. After at least one category has been created, you can add the value to the **Project Category** field.

- **Avatar**: There is a built-in set of images available for all projects. An initial avatar will be randomly defaulted to for your project when it is created. You can click on the **select image** link to change the avatar. On the ensuing screen, you can also upload a custom image from your computer. It is a required field.

- **Description**: The description provides users in our Jira instance with more information about the project. This field is optional.

- **Project Lead**: This is associated with the project lead role within the project. Typically, it refers to the main project administrator. This role can be used for additional permissions and notifications within the system. It is a required field.

- **Default Assignee**: All new issues created will be assigned to the default assignee if the field is populated. The only valid values are **Unassigned** or **Project Lead**. Individual users cannot be submitted for the field. If you want someone other than the project lead to be automatically assigned to new issues, you will need to change the value for the project lead.

You can change the values of the project's details at any time. After the changes are made, make sure that you click the **Save details** button.

People

For security reasons, you can change who has access to the project and what permissions they have by clicking on the **People** option on the left-hand menu, as shown in *Figure 3.15*. For instance, with the free subscription, all users automatically have access to all projects and are project administrators. For paid subscriptions, you can add multiple roles and users:

Figure 3.15 – Assigning access

For these paid subscription instances, the user should click on the **Add people** button in the upper-right corner. From there, you will be able to add users to the project and assign them to project roles.

Issue types

As demonstrated in the project template details, Jira Work Management projects are created with a predefined set of **issue types**. As we navigate to the issue types scheme, we can observe those issue types displayed in *Figure 3.16*:

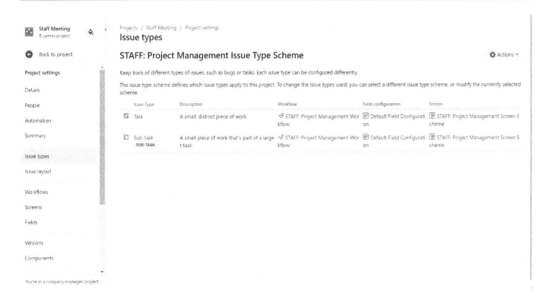

Figure 3.16 – Issue types

You can make changes to the list of issue types available for the project by clicking the **Issue types** option from the left-hand side menu. We will discuss this function in more detail in *Chapter 8, Configuring Permissions and Simple Administration*.

Screen and issue layout

The options to create, view, and edit **Screens** are available to enable users to control fields for issues on a project. They are a fascinating function in Jira with lots of caveats and complexities. They are the most common and effective way to view lots of information about a single issue in one place. Prior to the helpful inclusion of inline editable lists in Jira Work Management projects, screens were the only real way to update issues in Jira.

We will discuss how to create new custom fields in *Chapter 7, Managing Fields, Screens, and Issue Layouts*. However, if you would like to change the order of fields on a screen, you can do so in the following manner:

1. Select **Issue layout** from the menu on the left-hand side. It will display a screen that is similar to *Figure 3.17*.

2. Select the link for one of the screens in the middle of the display. In our preceding example, we have a single screen available for all the edit, view, and create functions:

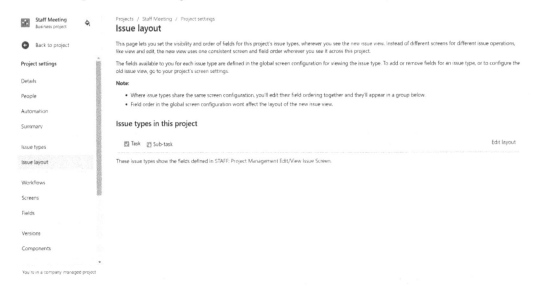

Figure 3.17 – Issue screens

The preceding **Issue layout** screen will actually show multiple screens by issue type if different screens have been created for different issue types.

> **Note**
> We will discuss how to create separate screens for the edit, view, and create functions in *Chapter 8, Configuring Permissions and Simple Administration*. Part of that discussion will be that you can have multiple screens per issue type. In other words, you can have a screen with certain fields on it for the **Task** issue type and a different screen with different fields for the **Sub-task** issue type. If that is the case, you will be able to observe separate rows for the screens and the issue type they are associated with on the view, as shown in *Figure 3.17*.

Again, to edit the screen, simply click on the link for the screen:

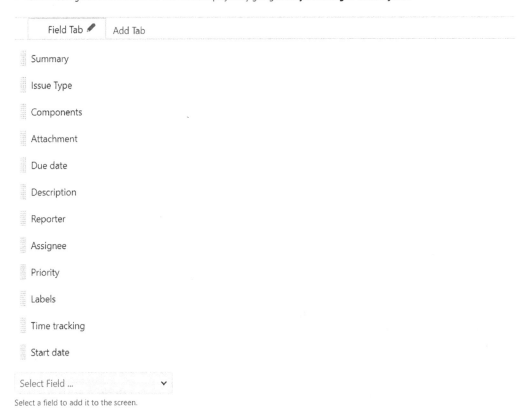

Figure 3.18 – Configuring the screen

At this point, the user can add existing fields to a screen or rearrange the order of the fields on the screen. This applies at an overall level for the screen, meaning that it will apply to all projects and issues that use this screen. When fields are added or rearranged, the screen is immediately saved.

Alternatively, you can make changes to the screen layout that only affect the project. While on the **Issue layout** screen, as shown in *Figure 3.17*, the user can select the issue layout link on the right-hand side of the issue types listing.

The issue layout functionality provides a mechanism to override the order and placement of fields for the attached screen, but just for this project. Remember how we mentioned any changes to the actual screen will be organization-wide? However, here, we can rearrange things a bit for just our project. Changing the order and placement of the fields here will not change the order of the fields on the screen for any other project:

Figure 3.19 – Issue layout

There are three major sections to the layout: **Description fields**, **Context fields**, and **HIDE WHEN EMPTY**. Fields can be dragged easily from one section to another, as desired, for better viewing. It should be noted that the changes applied to the issue layout will apply to all the user's views of the screen for that project. And again, this change can only be made by a project administrator.

Sometimes, there are fields present on the screen that are associated with the combination of project and issue type but are no longer desired to be seen. You can remove the fields from being visible for just this project by dragging the fields to the far-right section labeled **Hidden fields**. This can either be a temporary solution or a more permanent solution. Note that any changes you make to the issue layout must be saved by clicking on the **Save changes** button at the bottom of the screen.

When a new project is created, the default placement for fields in the issue layout is that paragraph or multiline fields will land in the **Description fields** section, while most other fields will be placed in the **Context fields** section. Finally, some system-level fields will be designated to the **HIDE WHEN EMPTY** section. These are hidden when empty fields include the following:

- Labels
- Original estimate
- Time tracking
- Components

If no separate view screen has been created, all the fields will be considered to be in *edit mode* when you enter the screen. Field values can be changed directly by entering values in the field. Less commonly used fields can be dragged to the bottom **HIDE WHEN EMPTY** section to not take up real estate on the screen. To access these fields while on the screen, click on the **More fields** drop-down menu in the bottom-right corner to display the fields:

Figure 3.20 – More fields

Often, we would like to apply this new issue layout for multiple projects. This could be for only some projects or perhaps even all projects. Making all the changes for several projects would be very cumbersome and frustrating. However, the issue layout feature has gone through several enhancements in the past few years that address that concern.

One of the best of these improvements is the ability to copy the issue layout and apply the layout to other projects. While this is still not ideal, it provides for a great interim step on the way to the issue layout functionality being implemented more like schemes in the future.

For now, simply click on the **Copy issue layout** button in the upper-right corner of the screen and then follow the prompts. It should be noted that you can only copy the layout to other projects that use the same screen.

Schemes

The concept of schemes is one of the most powerful features in Jira. It provides increased functionality and flexibility. However, it also brings increased complexity and frustration for new administrators. We will discuss this more fully in *Chapter 8, Configuring Permissions and Simple Administration*, but some mention of it needs to take place here.

You can think of a scheme as a bucket holding multiple items. So, a screen scheme can hold multiple screens in it – each performing different functions, such as edit, create, or view. A workflow scheme can hold multiple workflows – each associated with a different issue type and providing for varied paths across the board for each type.

Finally, it is the scheme that is attached to the project and not the individual items in the bucket. The bucket is attached to the project and, therefore, all the contents within the bucket apply to the project.

Workflows

Normally, workflows are a great example of the scheme concept. However, with Jira Work Management projects, only one workflow is allowed to be attached to the project for the built-in board to work. JWM projects still follow the scheme approach, even though only one workflow will probably be contained within the scheme bucket.

For the project administrator to view and/or make changes to the workflow for the Jira Work Management project, we begin by selecting the **Workflows** option from the left-hand side menu:

Figure 3.21 – Workflow scheme

The resulting page shows the contents of the bucket. In this case, the single project management workflow for the project. To edit the workflow, click on the pencil icon (**Edit**) on the far-right side. This leads us to the actual workflow. If the view of the workflow lands on the **Text** display of the workflow, it is best to click on the **Diagram** button to observe it in a visual rendering:

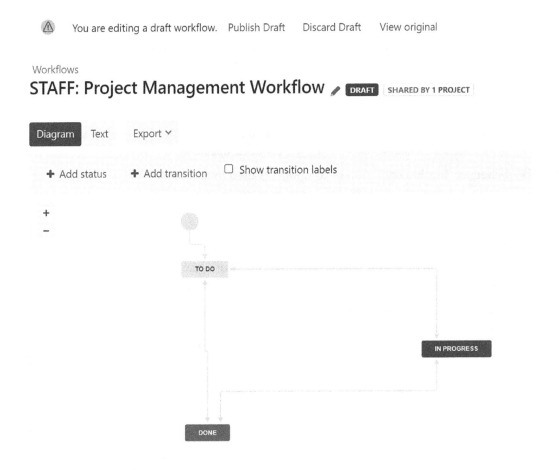

Figure 3.22 – Workflow

We will discover how to modify the workflow, and therefore the board, in *Chapter 4, Modifying the Board, Workflow, and Associated Schemes.*

New terms learned in this chapter

Let's conclude this chapter by going through the list of new terms we have learned:

- **Key**: This is the unique code to identify an issue or project.

- **Quickstart**: This is a guide within Jira Work Management that contains more in-depth information about the project.

- **Issue**: This is the Jira term for a unit of work to be done. It is also known as a card or a ticket.

- **Project settings**: This is the administration section that controls the functions of a project. You must be a project administrator to access this section of the project.

- **Screens**: This is the most used interface between a user and the information related to the work being performed.

- **Issue layout**: This is the administrative function of a project, which controls the order and sections of a screen in which the fields appear.

- **Schemes**: This is a collection of components used to administer various functions of a project. Schemes can be shared across projects.

Summary

Congratulations! You have now created your first Jira Work Management project. Hopefully, you have also discovered a few new issues/cards to go along with it.

In this chapter, we learned how easy it is to follow the template process to create a Jira Work Management project. We answered the question of what's next after project creation with our equally simple trip down the project settings path to the world of JWM project administration.

Armed with this new ability, you can now feel confident about accessing simple administration components that will give you more insight into your project and the work you are performing.

In the next chapter, we will jump into the details of how to modify the board and underlying workflow, how to create new boards, and how to interact with various schemes to give us real power over our Jira Work Management projects.

Section 2:
Enhancing Your
JWM Project

In this section, you will be able to extend the creation of a simple, initial project to a useful and robust means of doing work. You will learn how to take advantage of the newest JWM features to the fullest while joining existing Jira functionality.

This section contains the following chapters:

- *Chapter 4, Modifying the Board, Workflow, and Associated Schemes*
- *Chapter 5, JWM Toolset: Summary, List, Timeline, and the Calendar*
- *Chapter 6, Forms, Issues, Dashboards, and Reports*
- *Chapter 7, Managing Fields, Screens, and Issue Layouts*

4

Modifying the Board, Workflow, and Associated Schemes

You should have created your first project by now, and maybe even a few new issues for your work. You also have a good idea of how to find your way around the project settings world to do some simple administration, if nothing more than looking at what is initially set up.

Now it is time to dig deeper into how to make changes to the original objects created with the project template. Very few times will you just accept what gets created out of the box. Most likely, there will be several changes you want to make so that your project reflects more closely how you work in your organization or on your team.

For example, modifying transitions in the workflow can be done to simplify the options available to users, so they only see relevant statuses when moving from column to column. Or maybe you want to only allow a change in statuses when a field is not empty (meaning the field becomes required at some point in the workflow).

Whatever your need or motivation, this chapter will provide you with the necessary skills to make those modifications. As you make those changes and learn additional administration, you will see your productivity rise quickly.

In this chapter, we are going to cover the following main topics:

- Using the board
- Accessing and modifying the workflow
- The schemes used by **Jira Work Management (JWM)** projects
- Working with **Atlassian Marketplace** apps

By the end of this chapter, you will be able to identify the nuts and bolts of a JWM project board. You will understand how to add more columns to the board and how to arrange the order of those columns. This will be done in conjunction with modifying the workflow for the type of work you are accomplishing.

You will also be able to locate the schemes used to administer the JWM project and make simple changes to it. Finally, you will be able to explore and add some of the most used and powerful third-party apps available in the Atlassian Marketplace.

Technical requirements

As JWM is only available in the **Jira Cloud** environment, the requirement for this chapter is simple:

- Access to a Jira Cloud environment
- Access to an internet browser with the ability to navigate to the Atlassian Marketplace

If you already have access to Jira Cloud, that's great – you're ready to go! If not, Atlassian provides a free JWM account for up to 10 users. You can create your account by going to `https://www.atlassian.com/try/cloud/signup?bundle=jira-core&edition=free` and following the instructions.

Using the board

When managing software development or other technical projects, the **Kanban board** or **Sprint board** is the star of the show. Kanban simply wouldn't be Kanban without a board – either physical or digital/virtual. And Sprints are so much easier to manage when viewing the work on a board.

Often, this is also the case with business projects. Visually seeing the work you need to do or have completed and viewing the progress you have made is debatably best using a board. Now that JWM projects have implemented **inline editable lists**, the board has less significance, although it will still be the major interaction point for most users.

Lists will be covered in detail in *Chapter 5, JWM Toolset: Summary, List, Timeline, and the Calendar*, but for now, let's take a close look at the board.

Inherently, business projects will not use the **Scrum methodology** and therefore will not have Sprint boards available. And although the board that is automatically created when a project is created is not technically a Kanban board, it has many of the same attributes. But for JWM projects, we will simply call it the **board**.

As the development of the JWM product is still ongoing, you should expect to see some nice enhancements continue to be rolled out for the toolset, including the board. The images of the board shown in this book are the latest available at the time of publishing.

It is important to point out some of the differences between the JWM board versus Jira software project boards; we will look at some of these differences in more detail later in this section:

- By design, only one board is created for JWM projects. You can create additional Kanban boards and use issues from your JWM project, but you will lose the built-in connection to the project. We will explore how to do this in this chapter. As mentioned earlier, no Scrum or Sprint functionality exists; if you need to perform this type of work, you should create a Jira Software project.

- You cannot change the inner workings of the board – including what colors or fields are displayed.

- Columns are directly related to statuses in your workflow.

- Only one workflow is allowed for every issue type for the board to function.

Finding the board

To navigate to the board for any existing JWM project, we must begin by searching for the project:

1. Click on the **Projects** menu option in the top navigation bar and select your desired project if it is shown.

2. By design, Jira will show the last five projects that you have visited.

3. If you do not see the desired project, click on the **View all projects** link and search for the project.

The following screenshot shows how to search for an existing project:

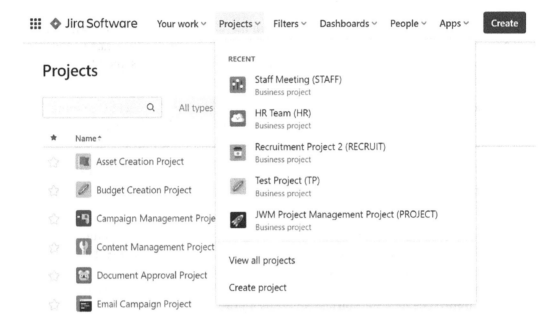

Figure 4.1 – Searching for the project

Whichever way you navigate to the project, the result will typically find you landing on the project board as seen in *Figure 4.2* in the next section.

Components of the board

If you are familiar with the boards created for Jira Software projects, the most glaring difference for business project boards is the lack of the **Board Settings** functionality. This has been true from the start of the JWM product precursor, Jira Core, and remains that way for the time being.

The result is that there is not a lot of functionality that you can change about the board. In this case, what you see is what you get, which makes things very simple. So, let's talk about the things that we do see, as shown in the following screenshot:

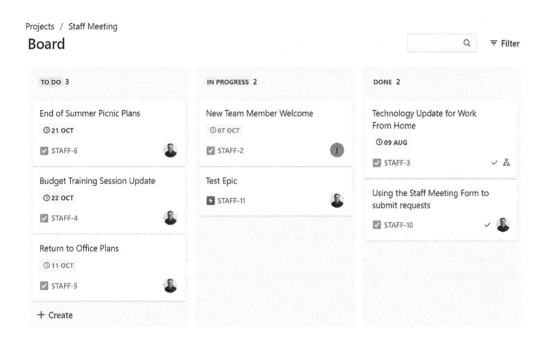

Figure 4.2 – The board

We will begin at the top of the board and work our way down:

- **Project name**: While on any JWM project board, you will see the name of the project displayed at the very top in the breadcrumbs section. Jira's philosophy is that you arrive at a board by first navigating through a project.

- **Search and filters**: Two search boxes can be seen while on the board screen. One exists all of the time in the top navigation bar, that box searches the entire Jira instance. The second is visible on the board and only searches for information on that board.

- **Columns**: Columns represent statuses in the project's workflow. There is a one-to-one relationship between the column and each status. Another way to say that is that every status in the workflow will appear as a column on the board. Statuses cannot be hidden on the board.

- **Cards**: Issues appear as cards on the board. The board will display only six pieces of information about the card:

  - The summary or title of the issue

  - The issue key (for example, STAFF-4)

  - The due date (if one exists for the issue)

- The assignee (if one exists for the issue)
- Resolution – this appears as a checkmark on the card if the card has a resolution
- Sub-task count (if any exist for the issue)

Functions of the board

At face value, the board exists to show what work you are doing on the project and the status of that work. Outside of viewing the cards, there is very little functionality of a JWM project board. But let's look at what can be done.

Changing the status

One function is that you can quickly change the status of an issue by simply dragging the card from one column to another. Which column you can move the card to depends on which transitions exist in the project's workflow. We discuss that in detail in a later section in this chapter.

Searching the board

The **search box** near the top of the board provides a quick way to find issues on the board based on issue text or the issue key. This is especially helpful when there are several dozen cards visible on the board. Simply begin by typing information into the search box and the functionality will automatically hide any cards that do not match what was typed in the box.

For example, typing 87 in the box will find any card on the board with a key that has the number 87, if one exists (STAFF-87, ID-870, and so on).

To search your entire Jira instance for an issue, click in the search box in the top navigation bard.

Filtering issues

There are two **QUICK FILTERS** available on the board at this time – **Assigned to me** and **Due this week**. As you might guess, clicking on the **Assigned to me** filter shows only the cards on the board that are currently assigned to you.

And clicking on **Due this week** will only show cards that have a value in the due date field and the value is this week. It should be noted that if the due date is past due, you will see the date displayed in the color red. For cards that have not reached the due date, the dates will display in black. Note that the year is not included, just the day and month:

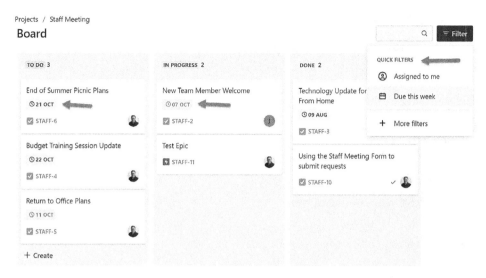

Figure 4.3 – Board with recent dates

Now that we are more familiar with our way around the board, let's see how we can add some work to it.

Creating an issue

Finally, as we discussed in *Chapter 3*, *Creating Your First Project*, you can create new issues directly on the board. To do that, click on the **Create** button at the bottom of the first column on the board, as shown in *Figure 4.3*. This will pop up a new box with the words **Start typing** visible.

Now that we have seen how to work with the standard board, let's explore how a second board can be created.

Creating a second board

First, let me note that this is more of an advanced step and definitely outside-of-the-box thinking. Because of that, this new board will not be accessible directly from the project as the built-in board is. We will understand this better after we have created the board.

So why would you want to create a second board? Mainly because the initial board created with your JWM project is not very customizable. With a second board, you can do the following:

- You can choose to name the board whatever you like.

- You can choose the board filter being used, which will give you better control of the issues displayed on the board.

- You can add your own quick filters to the board.
- You can control colors for the side panel of the cards on the board.
- You can control which fields are displayed on the card when viewing the board.
- You have more control as to who can even see the board.

To begin, perform the following steps:

1. Click the search box in the top navigation bar.
2. Select **Boards** at the bottom of the display.
3. Click on the **Create board** button.
4. Select Scrum or Kanban. Unless you are using Sprints (which is very rare for business projects), click the **Create a Kanban board** button.
5. Select the option for **Board from an existing project**. Then click **Next**.
6. Give the board a name and select the project to which you would like to add this new board.
7. For the **Location**, select **Personal** and then your username.
8. Finally, click on the **Create board** button.

For steps 7 and 8, your view will look something like *Figure 4.4*:

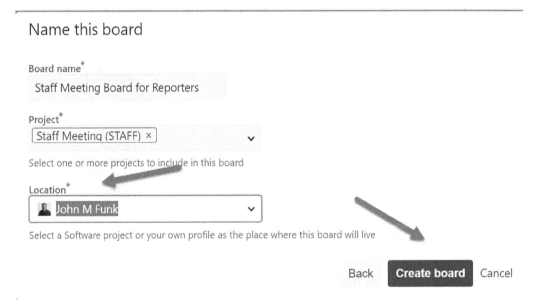

Figure 4.4 – Board location

It's the **Location** field that gives most administrators trouble. Since this is a second board outside the purview of the main JWM project board, Jira does not allow you to use any JWM project for the **Location** field. That means that you cannot select the board from the left-hand menu while you are on the board. This makes it very hard for other users to find the board. I have found that the best method is simply to bookmark the URL for the board in your browser and share the address with others.

Other users can also find the board by searching on the list of boards at `https://yourdomain.atlassian.net/jira/boards`, where `yourdomain` is the domain for your Jira instance.

Yes, it's a bit of trouble to get the board set up and to share it with others, but many administrators and users find the increased functionality of the second board to be worth it. To learn more about board creation process, you can see the guidance from Atlassian Support at `https://support.atlassian.com/jira-software-cloud/docs/create-a-board/`. And you can learn more about the board configuration process at `https://support.atlassian.com/jira-software-cloud/docs/configure-a-company-managed-board/`.

Next, we will see how to make changes to the project workflow.

Accessing and modifying the workflow

We saw the importance of workflows in *Chapter 2, Working with Project Templates*, and we explored how to access them in *Chapter 3, Creating Your First Project*. Now we will learn how to make changes to the workflow and how that affects the board.

As a review, you must be a project administrator or a Jira administrator to be able to make changes to the workflow used by the project. If the workflow is shared across multiple projects, you must be a Jira administrator to alter the shared workflow.

We will see how to share a workflow across multiple projects later in this section. For our initial purposes here, we will assume the workflow attached to the project is the original workflow created when we created the project and that it is not connected to any other project. Perform the following steps:

1. To access the project workflow scheme, you must first begin by clicking on **Project settings** in the lower options of the left menu:

Figure 4.5 – Project settings

2. Again, if you do not see the **Project settings** menu option, then you do not have project administrator permissions. Once inside the **Project settings** environment, click on the **Workflows** link on the left menu. This will display the workflow scheme attached to the project, as seen in *Figure 4.6*:

Figure 4.6 – Project workflow scheme

By default, JWM projects have only one workflow created for all issue types on the project. The workflow is present inside a workflow scheme, which is attached to the project. So, in our example in the preceding screenshot, **STAFF: Project Management Workflow Scheme** is the name of our workflow scheme. Note that **STAFF: Project Management Workflow** is indeed the name of our workflow and is associated with both the **Task** and **Sub-task** issue types.

The workflow text view

We can view the workflow in text form by clicking on the **View as text** link beside the workflow name, as shown in the preceding screenshot.

The text version is helpful primarily for seeing the relationships between statuses:

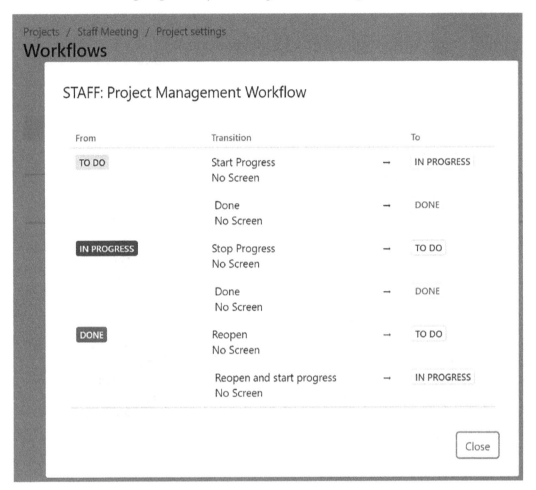

Figure 4.7 – Workflow text view

These relationships are called **transitions** in the Jira world and identify the statuses that issues can move to and from. These transitions appear as lines in the **diagram** version, which we see displayed in *Figure 4.8.*

To read the text version, the left side shows all of the statuses in the workflow. You can think of statuses as steps along the workflow path, and they appear as columns on the project board. The right-hand side shows the status that each of the left-hand statuses can move to. For instance, issues in the **TO DO** status can move to either the **IN PROGRESS** status or the **DONE** status.

The column in the middle shows the name of the transition that would be used to navigate to the desired next step or status. So, to move from the **TO DO** status to the **IN PROGRESS** status, you would use the **Start Progress** transition.

These transitions also make it known whether you can move from one status to another. If no transition exists between two statuses, it is not possible to move an issue between them. Our example in *Figure 4.7* is very straightforward in that all three statuses can move to both other statuses. This is not the case in all workflows. Some workflows follow a more linear path with steps that must be navigated in a rigid order.

Transitions will also determine which columns on a board that a card can move to. If no transition exists between the statuses, you will not be able to migrate a card from that column to the other column.

Finally, it is possible to add a screen that will pop up as you move from one status to another or one column to another. These screens are often referred to as transition screens. These screens typically have a small number of fields that often represent required data to move an issue between the steps. We will discuss these transition screens and how to add them later in this chapter.

The text version of the workflow will identify the name of the transition screen that is available or used between statuses if one exists. Otherwise, it will simply say **No Screen,** as shown in our example in *Figure 4.7*.

The workflow diagram view

If you click on the **View as diagram** link for the workflow, as shown in *Figure 4.6*, you will see a more visual view of the workflow, as shown in *Figure 4.8*:

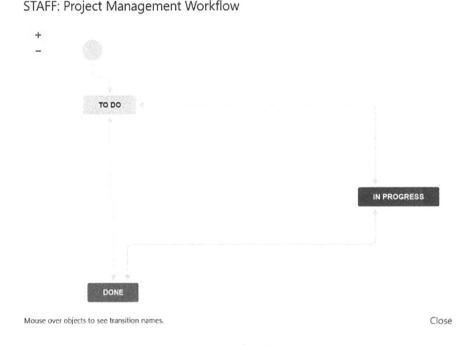

Figure 4.8 – Workflow diagram view

The diagram view is usually the easiest view to read and understand. The circle at the top represents the beginning of the workflow with the line from the circle to the first status (**TO DO** in this example) being known as the Create transition. The lines between the statuses, as mentioned earlier, represent the transitions between the statuses.

The arrows at the ends of the lines show the direction in which an issue might move from one status to the other. So, a line with arrows at both ends means that issues can move back and forth between the two statuses. In reality, these are two different transitions with each going in a singular direction. They just happen to overlap in the diagram as produced by the project template. We can see an example of the dual transition lines in *Figure 4.11*.

Look at the note in the bottom left of *Figure 4.8* that states **Mouse over objects to see transition names**. The objects it is referring to are the lines between the statuses in the diagram. To zoom in or out on the diagram, simply click the + or – buttons in the top left of the view.

Clicking either of the links to **View as text** or **View as diagram** as described earlier will show the workflows in a read-only mode – you cannot change the workflow using either of these links. To make changes to the workflow, click the pencil icon under **Actions** on the right-hand side of the workflow scheme view, as shown in *Figure 4.6*.

The workflow edit mode

Edit mode will show the workflow in either the **Diagram** or **Text** interface. This will allow you to make changes to the workflow. Notice in *Figure 4.9* that we have entered **Diagram** edit mode. We also have clicked on the box to **Show transition labels**:

Issues

You are editing a draft workflow.   Publish Draft   Discard Draft   View original

Workflows
STAFF: Project Management Workflow ✏ DRAFT SHARED BY 1 PROJECT

Diagram   Text   Export ⌄

+ Add status   **+** Add transition   ☑ Show transition labels

+
−

Create
TO DO ←──── Stop Progress

Start Progress

Reopen

IN PROGRESS

Done   Done   Reopen and start progress

DONE

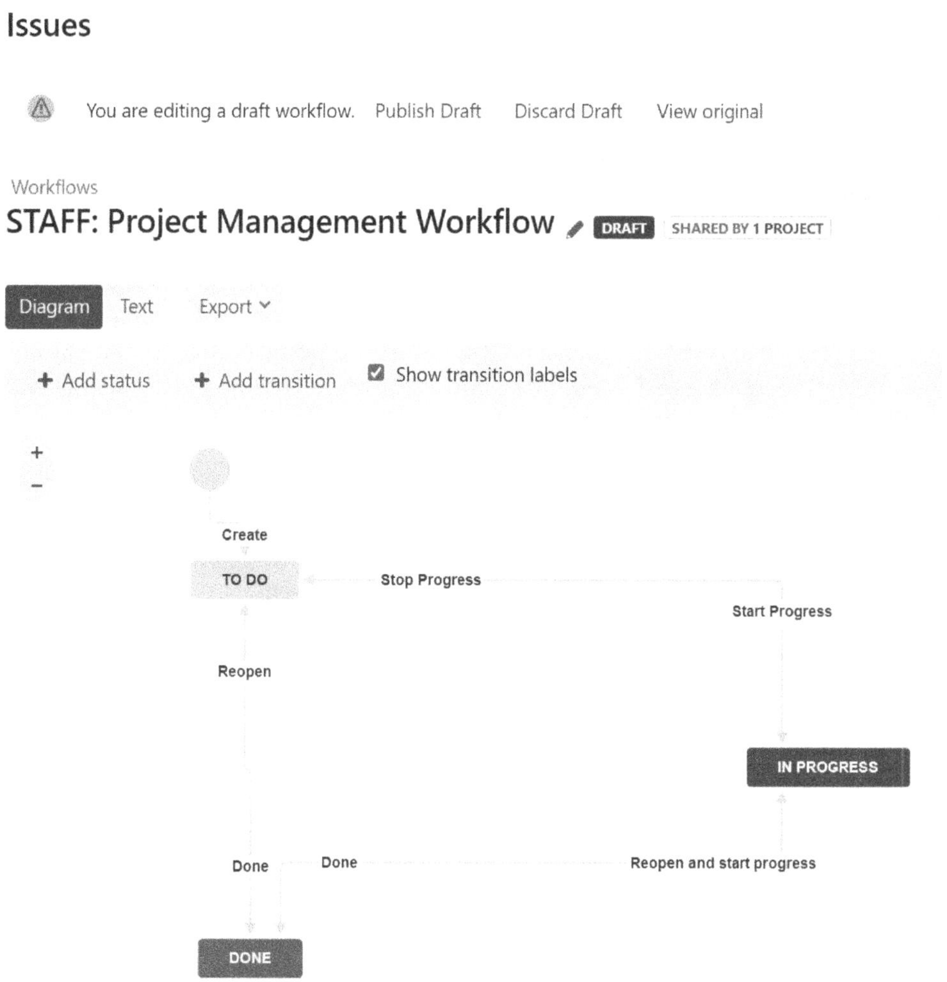

Figure 4.9 – Workflow Diagram edit mode with transition names

Notice how the transition names match the names as displayed in the **View as text** image, as shown in *Figure 4.7*. Also, you will see the statement **You are editing a draft workflow** because we entered in edit mode. At this point, you can make changes and then save the modifications by clicking on the **Publish Draft** link near the top of the page, or you can dispose of the modifications by clicking the **Discard Draft** link. Or you can view the original as it was when you first created the workflow.

Although there is a pencil icon next to the name of the workflow, you are not allowed to change the name here. Clicking the icon will open a dialog box that enables you to add a *description* for the workflow. Adding a description will display the entered text just below the workflow name.

Editing the workflow

At this point, we can make changes to the workflow in a variety of ways. First, let's look at the transitions. As mentioned earlier, in our example, there are two transitions between every two statuses. That makes it much harder to edit individual transitions or to even clearly see that there is more than one.

Clicking on one of the lines will reveal a pop-up box to the right of the diagram. Since the **Stop Progress** transition is on top of the **Start Progress** transition, when you click on the line, only the **Stop Progress** transition can be edited at this point. Notice that the **Stop Progress** transition name is displayed in the pop-up box and is shown inside a gray box on the line:

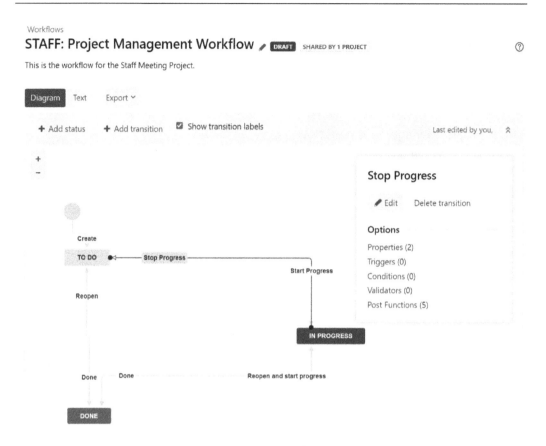

Figure 4.10 – Editing workflow transitions

When you select a transition, you will see a small black dot displayed at each end of the line. These dots will allow you to click on the end of the line and drag it to another circle on the same status or on another status. This will separate the two lines so that you can now edit the underlying **Start Progress** transition:

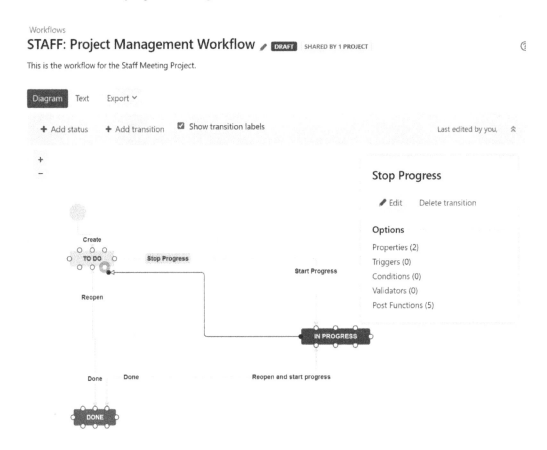

Figure 4.11 – Moving workflow transitions

When the dot is released, the **Stop Progress** name will shift to be on the new location of the transition line. *Figure 4.12* shows the result after all the transitions have been moved to provide more clarity:

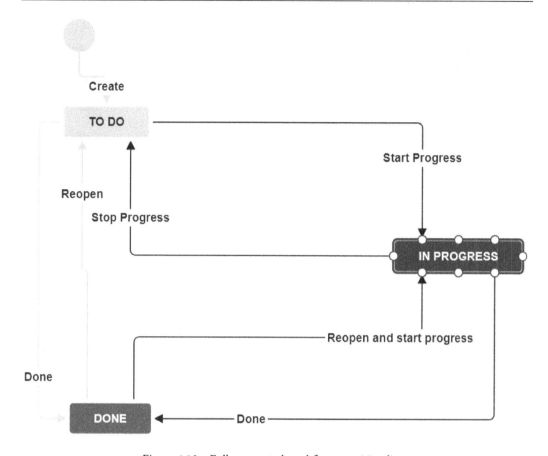

Figure 4.12 – Fully separated workflow transition lines

To change the name of the transition, perform the following steps:

1. Click on the line for the transition you want to change.

2. Click on the **Edit** button in the pop-up box on the right-hand side.

3. Change the name of the transition by changing the text in the **Name** field.

4. This is also the point where you can add a transition screen to the transition. The screen must have already been created before linking it to the transition at this point.

5.   Simply click on the **Screen** drop-down box and select the screen:

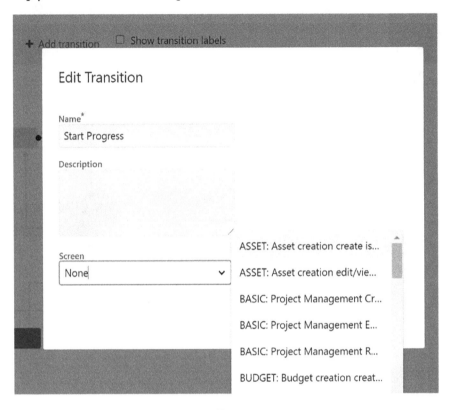

Figure 4.13 – Transition screen

Triggers, conditions, validators, and post functions can add a lot of power to the workflow. Executing a transition will cause each of these items to fire in the order listed. Brief descriptions of what each function provides are listed here:

- **Trigger**: Causes events to happen in your connected development tools
- **Condition**: Controls whether the transition is visible to the user
- **Validator**: Checks that entered data is correct before allowing the transition to continue
- **Post function**: Performs additional processes such as setting values of fields, sending emails, auto-transitioning, and adding comments

Atlassian's own document provides good guidance about each of these functions. You can see that guidance at `https://support.atlassian.com/jira-cloud-administration/docs/configure-advanced-issue-workflows/`.

Adding statuses

For our Staff Meeting Project, let's say we want to add a new column to our project board. The intention is to bring more clarity about which presentations are still being prepared, which presentations have been finished and added to the agenda for the next staff meeting, and which presentations have been completely presented and are considered done.

For the new column to be added to the board, we must first add a new status to the workflow:

1.   We enter **Diagram** edit mode for the workflow as described earlier.

2.   Then we click on the **Add status** button in the row just above the diagram.

It should be noted that when we add a new status to the workflow, we can select from existing statutes already available in our Jira instance, or we can create and save an entirely new status for our organization to use. In the dialog box, we will enter **On Agenda** for the new status name:

Figure 4.14 – Adding a workflow status

Because the **On Agenda** status does not already exist for our organization, we see the words **(new status)** added next to our text. This is an informational note that we must create this new status for our Jira instance before it can be used. You must click on the **On Agenda (new status)** text for the system to recognize that you are indeed adding a new status to your instance. Then click the **Add** button.

The ensuing pop-up box allows us to select one of the three status categories for our new status – **To Do**, **In Progress**, or **Done**. Since **On Agenda** represents work that is not completely done yet, we will choose **In Progress** for the **Category**:

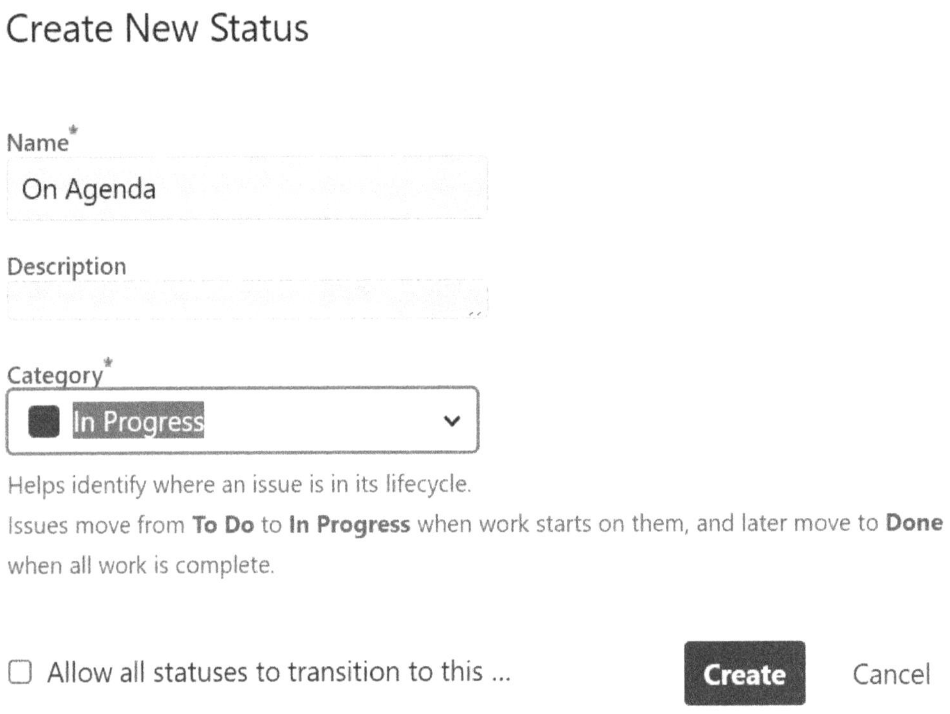

Create New Status

Name*

On Agenda

Description

Category*

In Progress   ⌄

Helps identify where an issue is in its lifecycle.

Issues move from **To Do** to **In Progress** when work starts on them, and later move to **Done** when all work is complete.

☐ Allow all statuses to transition to this ...   **Create**   Cancel

Figure 4.15 – Choosing a status category

We also can add a **Description** for the new status at this stage if we choose. Finally, we could select the box for **Allow all statuses to transition to this status** if the workflow should allow an issue to move to this status from any other status in the workflow. We will leave the box unchecked in this case since the **On Agenda** status path is more linear in nature.

After the status is added to the diagram, we will need to connect the new status to the existing **IN PROGRESS** status. We can do that by two different methods. One is by clicking on the **IN PROGRESS** status and dragging a new line to the **ON AGENDA** status:

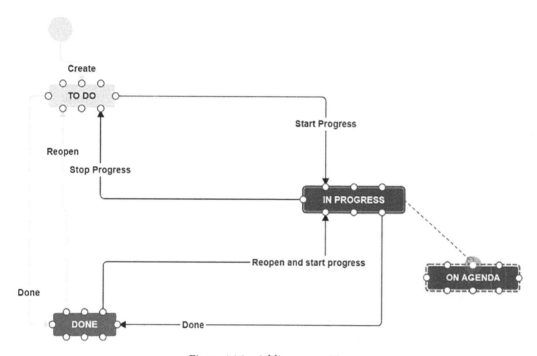

Figure 4.16 – Adding a transition

The result will be a dialog box that pops up to allow you to name the new transition. We will call this new transition `Move to On Agenda`:

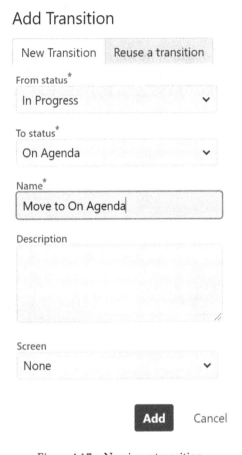

Figure 4.17 – Naming a transition

Be sure to click the **Add** button to save the transition and add it to the workflow. The second way to add a new transition is to click on the **Add transition** button as seen in *Figure 4.14*.

For our second transition, we will add a transition from the new **ON AGENDA** status to the existing **DONE** status. However, in this case, we will reuse an existing transition that already goes to **DONE**. The primary reason to do this is that it potentially saves a large amount of time by not having to add any conditions, validators or post functions to a transition. It will make use of the functionality already in place when moving to the **DONE** status. Also, if you need to modify the transition, it only needs to be changed in a single location and have it applied to all the same transitions going to the **DONE** status.

> **Note**
>
> You must publish the draft workflow that contains your changes for the changes to be applied to your production instance.

Finally, as we return to the project board, we see that the new **ON AGENDA** status has been automatically added as a column to the board:

Figure 4.18 – Board view with new status

Next, we will take a look at other schemes that are available for the administration of JWM projects.

The schemes used by JWM projects

To use a metaphor, the project board and screens are like the body of a car – the shiny and sleek visual of what most of us actually identify as being the car. It's what we see and touch and show others. But under that JWM car is the chassis or frame, made up of schemes that set our permissions, control notifications and type of work, and provide the workflow, among other things.

The best place to see the grouping of schemes is in the **Summary** of **Project settings**. To navigate there, click on **Project settings** while on the project and then select **Summary**. Remember, you must be a project administrator to access and change project settings such as schemes:

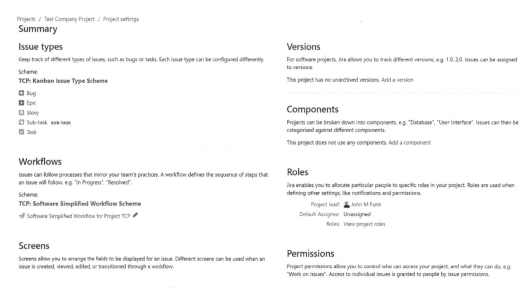

Figure 4.19 – Project settings summary

Do not get too caught up in trying to read the fine print in *Figure 4.19*; we will discuss the major headings. We should also note that this is just a cursory introduction to the schemes. We will learn how to modify them in more detail in *Chapter 8, Configuring Permissions and Simple Administration.*

Some of this information has been covered in previous chapters; however, it is good to see the schemes listed in an easy, summarized visual where scheme purposes can be compared. To get started, let's review the concept of schemes.

We mentioned in *Chapter 3, Creating Your First Project,* that schemes are like buckets that hold individual items related to the bucket. For instance, the **screen scheme** bucket will hold a set of screens used by the project. The **workflow scheme** will hold a set of workflows used by the project, and so on.

Some schemes are at a project level and have no components underneath them. They apply to all issues on the project, regardless of the issue type. Other schemes are related to issue types and are more granular, and thus can contain one or several underlying components. Let's take a look at the list, beginning with the project-level schemes:

- **Issue type scheme**: This scheme contains the list of issue types available for use in the project. All issues created on the project must be related to one of the issue types in the scheme. Since it is inherently a list of issue types, it operates at the project level and not the issue type level.

- **Permission scheme**: This scheme contains all permissions for the project, which control access to the project by users and what they are allowed to do when interacting with the project. It uses project roles, individual usernames, and/or groups to whom permissions may be granted. It operates at the project level.

- **Notification scheme**: This scheme identifies to whom and under what circumstances notifications are sent. Most of the notifications involve the creation of or changes to issues but will also address worklog or time tracking changes. It controls both emails and in-application notifications. It operates at the project level.

- **Issue security scheme**: This scheme controls who can see what issues are in the project. Multiple levels can be made available for the project, but only one level can be applied to each issue. Since there is no field-level security available in Jira, this is the most granular security level that can be applied. The scheme operates at the project level.

- **Workflow scheme**: Workflows identify the path that an issue can take from its creation until its final resolution. There can be multiple workflows related to a scheme and each workflow must be related to one or more issue types. For JWM projects, only a single workflow is allowed within the scheme for the project board to function properly. The scheme operates at the issue type level.

- **Screen scheme**: This scheme provides a list of screens available for the project. There can be three different types of screens in the scheme – **create, edit, and view**. One screen type is considered the default. The screen scheme must be attached to an issue type screen scheme, which identifies screens at the issue type level. Therefore, the scheme operates at the issue type level.

- **Issue type screen scheme**: This scheme identifies which screen schemes are attached to a single or multiple issue type. Therefore, you can have a separate create screen for each issue type, a separate edit screen for each issue type, and so on. Of course, it does not have to be broken down to this level. You can have a single screen that performs all functions – **create, edit, and view** – for all issue types. This is the out-of-the-box configuration for JWM projects. The scheme operates at the issue type level.

- **Field configuration scheme**: This scheme controls which fields are required when creating a new issue on a project. You can have separate field configuration files for each issue type, meaning each issue type can have different required fields when creating an issue. The field configuration file also controls the description for a field along with the type of rendering for text fields. This scheme operates at the issue type level.

> **Note**
>
> All of the following schemes will automatically be created when you create a new JWM project. And each scheme can be modified by a project or Jira administrator, except for the permission scheme for free subscriptions.

Working with Atlassian Marketplace apps

Atlassian has long been known for the capability of its products. Whether it is the flagship products of the Jira family or some of the more recent acquisitions of other tools, Atlassian has gathered a quite impressive collection of productivity-enhancing applications.

And as wonderful as this group of products has been and continues to be, Atlassian also extends the capabilities of Jira to even higher heights with the availability of products from third-party vendors through the Atlassian Marketplace. These are companies and applications that have been vetted by Atlassian and are available for additional purchase or maybe even for free!

One of the nice accompaniments of the Marketplace is that Atlassian will handle the billing for and collection of payment for the use of tools provided by these vendors. So, you get a single bill, either monthly or annually, that includes your Atlassian products – such as JWM, and any third-party apps.

Another amazing piece of trivia is that some of the products inside Atlassian started as Marketplace apps and were acquired by Atlassian over the years. Some of the more recent and most noticeable tools have been **Automation for Jira** and **ProForma Forms**. While the incorporation of Forms is still taking place, Automation has been a mainstay for many Jira users for the past couple of years.

As a by-product of their acquisitions, many of the tools are offered either for free with Jira's Standard pricing subscription or with the Premium subscription. So, let's highlight a couple. Both tools provide some similar functionality and are highly rated apps as Atlassian Platinum Marketplace Partners that have earned Atlassian's **Cloud Fortified** rating for security, reliability, and support response time.

Jira Miscellaneous Workflow Extensions by Innovalog Atlassian Apps

Known by the acronym of **JMWE**, the tool's company, Innovalog, was acquired by Atlassian solution provider powerhouse **Appfire** in 2020. JMWE extends Jira's out-of-the-box workflow function with powerful, yet easy-to-use, enhancements for conditions, validators, and post functions.

Much of this functionality requires no coding so that the user can be productive immediately. Point and click your way to automated business processes in the blink of an eye. Or for even more capability, add some code through easy scripting functionality to build your conditions or validators for complex needs.

See the Marketplace listing here and take advantage of a free trial: `https://marketplace.atlassian.com/apps/292/jira-misc-workflow-extensions-jmwe?hosting=cloud&tab=overview`.

ScriptRunner for Jira by Adaptavist

Long one of the favorites in the Atlassian Marketplace, **ScriptRunner** is also one of the most recommended tools by fellow Jira users.

ScriptRunner makes use of Groovy scripts and advanced JQL to enhance and automate workflows while extending Jira usage.

While having a coding background will be a tremendous help in navigating the tool, you will find it is unmatched in the power and control you receive. The unique set of available JQL functions allows you to create filters that ordinary searches would never be able to do. This includes bulk update functionality that allows you to save tons of time.

Sign up for a free trial or learn more about ScriptRunner for Jira at `https://marketplace.atlassian.com/apps/6820/scriptrunner-for-jira?hosting=cloud&tab=overview`.

Other apps

The Atlassian Marketplace offers hundreds of apps representing a plethora of functionality. There are apps for cloning, capturing time logs and reporting, calendars, email and notifications, checklists, and many, many more. You can see the full list for Cloud at `https://marketplace.atlassian.com/search?hosting=cloud`.

New terms learned in this chapter

Let's conclude the chapter by going through the list of new terms learned in this chapter:

- **Trigger**: Causes events to happen in your connected development tools.
- **Condition**: Controls whether the transition is visible to the user.
- **Validator**: Checks that entered data is correct before allowing the transition to continue.
- **Post function**: Performs additional processes such as setting values of fields, sending emails, auto-transitioning, and adding comments.
- **Inline editable lists**: Lists of issues where many, if not all, of the fields in the issue can be edited in the list view without opening the full issue detail view.
- **Quick filters**: Simple filters that are easily accessible to the user directly on the list view or board.
- **Location**: A system field associated with a company-managed project board designating which project the board will be visible under. JWM projects will use the user's profile instead.
- **Atlassian Marketplace**: A website where free and paid third-party apps that help extend the functionality of Jira are available.

Summary

As we have seen, there's no better way to get started with your new project than by adding issues to your project board and starting to manage your work.

In this chapter, we have learned how to modify the board and underlying workflow, providing us with enhanced flexibility to better adapt to how we do work in our organization. Now you don't have to settle for out-of-the-box functionality; you can modify it to meet your needs and extend your productivity.

We are also now familiar with JWM schemes and understand how to adjust them to give us more control of our project. And to give us even more power, we learned how Atlassian Marketplace apps such as JMWE and ScriptRunner can be added to the already excellent Jira family of products to produce even bigger and better results.

In the next chapter, we will begin to explore the new components that have come with the JWM rebranding, such as the List, Calendar, and Timeline. These are some of the newest and most exciting tools in the Jira toolset.

5
JWM Toolset: Summary, List, Timeline, and the Calendar

It has taken us a little while to get here, but now we get to view some of the new and wonderful tools that come with **Jira Work Management** (**JWM**) projects. We will look at these throughout this chapter and the next to give us ample time to see how each tool functions.

There was a lot of marketing by Atlassian surrounding JWM when it first rolled out, and they are continuing to do a great job with updates to the product by fixing any initial bugs and deploying additional enhancements to the features.

Now is the perfect time to try out the product if you haven't already. Refer to previous chapters to get your first project created and then add some issues, and as we progress through this chapter, see the real power by interacting with several or even all of the components we discuss.

In this chapter, we are going to cover the following main topics:

- The features of JWM
- Issues and their relationship to the JWM features
- JWM **Summary** section
- Using the **List**
- Working with the **Timeline**
- Adding issues to the **Calendar**
- New terms learned in this chapter

Upon completion of this chapter, you will have learned which features are available in JWM and how to interact with the **List**, **Timeline**, and **Calendar** functionality. You will also understand the intention of the **Summary** section and how the data gets populated.

Technical requirements

As JWM is only available in the **Jira Cloud environment**, the requirement for this chapter is simple: *access to a Jira Cloud environment.*

If you already have access to Jira Cloud, that's great—you are ready to go! If not, Atlassian provides a free JWM account for up to 10 users. You can create your account by going to `https://www.atlassian.com/try/cloud/signup?bundle=jira-core&edition=free` and following the instructions.

The features of JWM

Now, after all of the fanfare, we get to see the features. A list of components is available on the left-hand menu directly under the project name, as illustrated in the following screenshot:

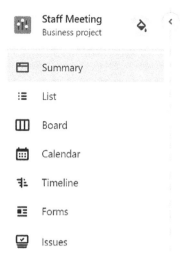

Staff Meeting
Business project

Summary

List

Board

Calendar

Timeline

Forms

Issues

Figure 5.1 – List of components

We'll now provide a quick description of the components, but we will delve more fully into each one in the coming sections. Every feature has been created with a specific purpose in mind and provides functionality that is different from the others. Remember that most of these tools are only available for JWM projects:

- **Summary**: The **Summary** section is just that. It provides you with a summary of activities that have been happening in your project, along with some key statistics.

- **List**: The **List** is already a fan favorite and provides a listing of all issues in your project. The ingenious part is that each column includes inline editing.

- **Board**: The **Board** has existed for quite some time, and although it is not new, there is some new functionality associated with it. It provides you with an easy-to-use **Kanban-style** view of your issues, presented as cards.

- **Calendar**: The **Calendar** presents issues as items on the calendar but includes interactive links, allowing you direct access to issues.

- **Timeline**: A **Timeline** is a roadmap or **Gantt-style** view of issues in your project, but this view also provides interactive functionality right on the timeline.

- **Forms**: At the time of writing this book, there was just one form available, but the **Forms** component comes with easy-to-create functionality and allows users, exterior to or within your project, to quickly create new issues or requests.

- **Issues**: As with the **Board**, this is an existing feature but provides functionality not seen elsewhere on projects. Also, it allows you to create filters and view the results in a list or as a single issue.

Now that we are aware of the new features, let's see what the relationship looks like between the features and the issues we create to capture our work.

Issues and their relationships to the JWM features

JWM features are just a viewset of issues we have created and identify the work we need to do. Issues then relate to the various tools in their unique ways, but since issues are the main element that describes the work that we do, the features are individually developed with that functionality in mind—in other words, each feature provides an enhanced method of interacting with the issues. That then leads us to select the feature best suited to how we want to work with a set of issues.

So, we once again provide a list of features here and identify their relationships to issues:

- **Summary**: Issues are shown in the context of changes that are happening to the issue. This is seen as an activity stream or as statics in aggregate form for the details of the issues. The information is view-only.

- **List**: A simple list of all the issues in your project, which can be reduced by applying filters. It also allows you to edit an issue directly inline in the list.

- **Board**: The classic Kanban view—displaying the issue as a card on the board with selected information visible. It also shows you a graphical representation of where each issue is at in terms of the workflow for the project—whether it has just been started or is close to being done. This is view-only, and you must click on the card to be able to edit it.

- **Calendar**: The calendar is view-only and consists of a monthly display of issues by **Due Date**. You must click on an individual issue to be able to edit it.

- **Timeline**: As already mentioned, this is a roadmap-type view of your issues. You can adjust the start or end date of an issue directly on the **Timeline** or add dependencies, but no other data is editable. You must click on the **Issue** key to be able to make additional changes.

- **Forms**: A form is just an intake layout for new work that provides an easy means to create new issues. You cannot view any issues while in a form—it is for creation only.

- **Issues**: This view provides a myriad of ways to interact with issues. While in **List** view mode, you can change the status of an issue but no other information. **Detail** view mode allows you to change all fields that appear on the edit screen for your project. The following screenshot shows how to select these view modes:

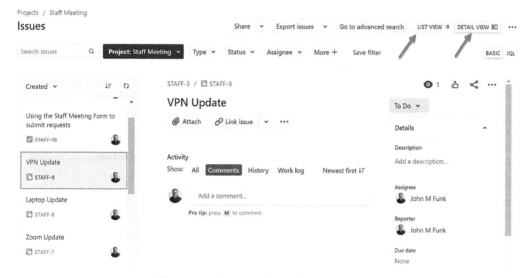

Figure 5.2 – Issues: LIST and DETAIL views

In the following sections, we will begin our discussion of some of the features. The **Board** was already covered in *Chapter 4, Modifying the Board, Workflow, and Associated Schemes*, and some features will be covered in *Chapter 6, Forms, Issues, Dashboards, and Reports*.

JWM Summary section

The **Summary** section is our first unique JWM feature to discuss. However, it can be seen as a compilation of existing functionality placed together to provide helpful insight into your project, and if you have previously used dashboards in Jira, this probably has a similar feel to you. As mentioned previously, we will further explore dashboards in our next chapter, *Chapter 6, Forms, Issues, Dashboards, and Reports*.

As you might guess, the **Summary** section is intended to give you a quick overview of what's happening with your project. The 30,000-feet-view cliché is a good one to apply here. The feature is broken into two sections: **Activity** and **Statistics**. Each is presented as a link and a tab-like format directly under the summary name.

If you have added a description to your project, it will appear between the **Activity** and **Statistics** links and the activity feed. Project lead and project key information is presented to the right, parallel to the project description, as illustrated in the following screenshot:

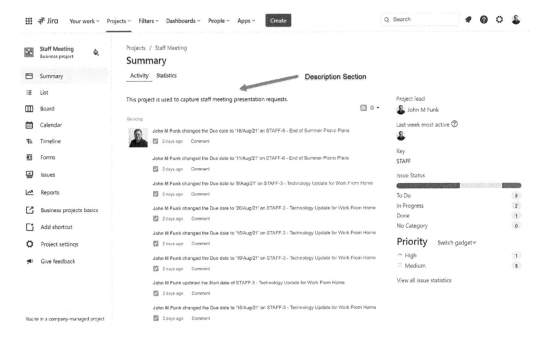

Figure 5.3 – Summary section with description

Activity

The large collection of historical information presented under the project description is similar, if not identical, to the activity feed gadget used in dashboards. Its purpose is to provide you with an easy-to-read flow of all activity that is happening on all issues in the JWM project, and it saves having to read through dozens or even hundreds of emails that get sent to **watchers**.

The activity information appears in chronological order, with the most recent history being displayed at the top. Events or changes are grouped by the day on which they happened. If the activity occurred within the last week, you see headings such as **Today**, **Monday**, or **Friday**. Events older than one week will be grouped with the date of the occurrence, such as **August 09** or **July 31**. You can see an overview of this in the following screenshot:

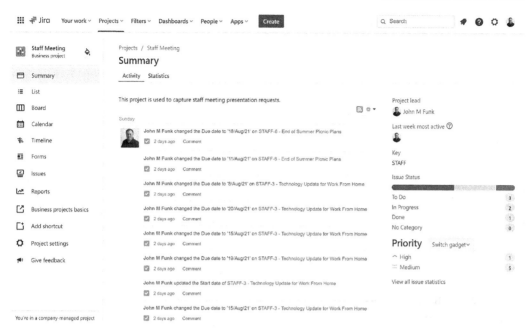

Figure 5.4 – Summary activity

The data shown is static based on the last refresh of the information. To do a new refresh, click on the gear icon to the right at the top of the list and then click on **Refresh**, as seen in the following screenshot. You can also see an **Extensible Markup Language** (XML) feed for the activity data by clicking on the **Feed** icon to the left of the **Refresh** icon. To get back to the **Summary** section, simply click the back button on your browser:

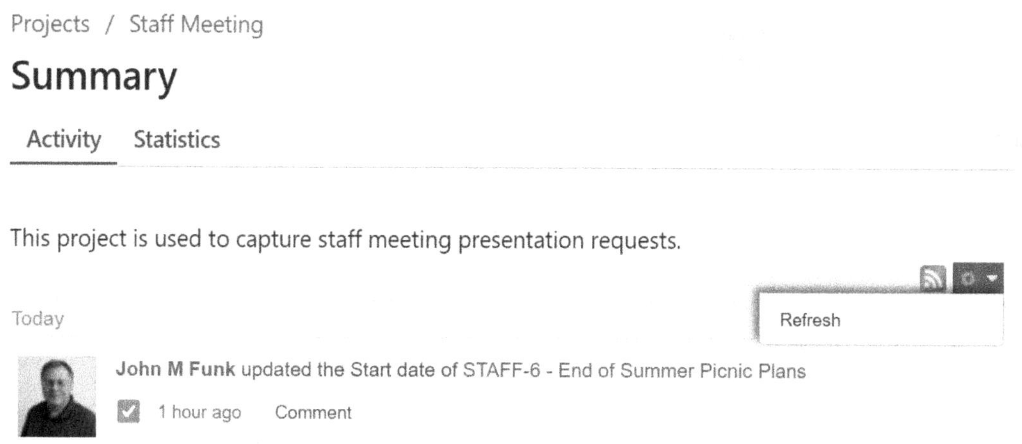

Projects / Staff Meeting

Summary

Activity   Statistics

This project is used to capture staff meeting presentation requests.

Today

John M Funk updated the Start date of STAFF-6 - End of Summer Picnic Plans

☑ 1 hour ago   Comment

Refresh

Figure 5.5 – Summary activity refresh

There is a small amount of statistical data also available on the **Activity** tab view on the right-hand side below the project lead and key information. The top section will show a grouping of the issues in your project based on the current status of each issue.

This information is similar to the **Issue Statistics** gadget that is available for dashboards (with **Status** as the issue statistic). The colored bar (grayscale in the printed book version) depicts a banded visual of the number in each status in relation to the other statuses. Hovering over each band will show you the number of issues in that status.

Each status name is a link that, if clicked on, will take you to the standard organization-wide search function for your Jira instance. It will present issues matching the number for that status in the **Jira Issues** view. That view will be discussed more in *Chapter 6, Forms, Issues, Dashboards, and Reports*. To get back to the **Summary** section, click the **Back** button on your browser.

Below the **Issue Status** section is another issue statistic gadget—the primary one is for **Priority**. In a similar fashion as with statuses, this gadget will show you a grouping of issues by their current priority. Clicking on the priority name will take you to the same standard **Jira Issues** view noted previously.

Finally, you can switch this bottom section to an additional gadget grouping of **Unresolved Issues by Assignee**. The same functionality applies to this gadget as well. Since this bottom section includes a dropdown, expect additional gadgets to be available in the future.

Statistics

Next, let's take a look at the **Statistics** tab. This display provides much of the same information as in the **Activity** view but in more of a dashboard-type view, as illustrated in the following screenshot. There is also a section at the top with several built-in filters related to the issues in your project. Clicking any of these takes you to the standard **Jira Issues** view:

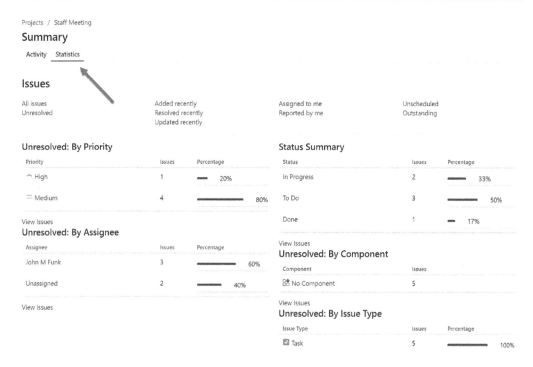

Figure 5.6 – Summary statistics

As you can see from the preceding screenshot, having a good summary available to see what is going on with your project at a high level can be very helpful, and since it is a top-level menu item, it is easy to find.

Next, we will begin interacting with features that we can use to make changes to our issues and to have them displayed in a variety of formats. First up will be the **List**.

Using the List

The **List** is one of the most exciting new features and provides fantastic new functionality. While it appears to be very similar to the standard **Jira Issues** view, the JWM **List** is unique in that all the columns provide inline editing functionality.

This new feature rivals the **queue** capabilities of the **Jira Service Management** (**JSM**) product as that tool's primary view of multiple issues. No board is created with JSM projects, and as JSM is mainly intended to be a ticketing-type system, agents rely heavily on the various queues available.

For JWM projects, however, the **List** provides an alternative view to the **Board**, along with enhanced editing capabilities directly in the tool. The feature is still under development, but I think you will find this to be a very welcome addition to the standard Jira functionality.

To access the **List**, simply click on the **List** menu option to the left. The **List** will display a set of columns matching the system fields available for the project. There is one column per field displayed. The default list of fields includes the following in order, from left to right:

- **Type**
- **Key**
- **Summary**
- **Status**
- **Assignee**
- **Due date**
- **Priority**
- **Labels**
- **Created**
- **Updated**
- **Reporter**

You can see an overview of some of these fields in the following screenshot:

Figure 5.7 – List

As you can see in *Figure 5.7*, only about half of the fields will be visible when you come into the display. You will need to use the scroll bar at the bottom of the list to see the additional fields to the right.

Changing columns

So, what if you don't want to see all those system fields in your **List** view? What if you want to see some of your custom fields displayed instead? Well, there's good news—the answer to both questions is: *You can!*

To control which columns appear in your list, click on the + icon to the far right in the heading list. This will result in a dropdown showing all available fields for the list (see *Figure 5.8*). The system fields will be shown first, followed by any custom fields you have created toward the bottom.

Not all custom field types are available to be used with the **List** at this time. However, most custom field types are already available. Be sure to scroll down to see all of the fields available. You will be able to rearrange the order of the columns on your list after you have added them to the list.

To add or remove a field from the list view, simply click on or click off the checkbox. The result will be immediate as you click each box. You can see an overview of this in the following screenshot:

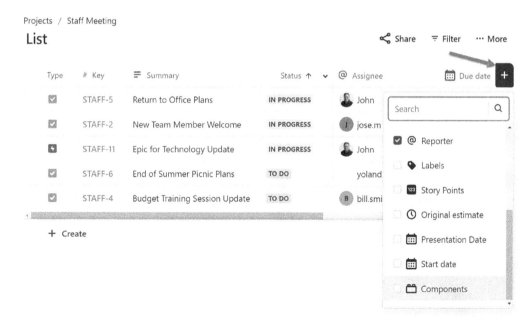

Figure 5.8 – Adding a column

Next, we will look at how to change the order of the columns.

Changing the order of columns

To change the order of columns on your list, simply click on the icon to the left of the column name and drag the column to the right or left. You will not be able to move the initial column for the issue type.

Resizing columns

As you add or remove columns/fields, it might be evident that some columns are displayed as wider than is desired. If that is the case, you can resize the width of the column by clicking on the line that separates the fields while in the header rows. This will highlight the line from top to bottom and you can slide it to the left or right to resize the column. Clicking outside of the line will set it. The following screenshot demonstrates how to resize a column:

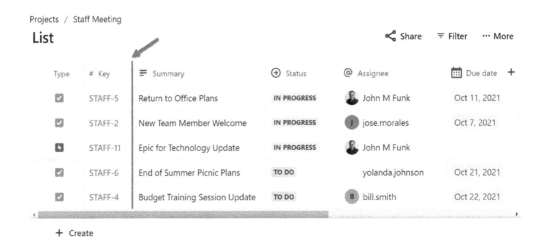

Figure 5.9 – Resizing a column

Now that some formatting of the list has been accomplished, let's take a look at other capabilities.

Inline editing

As we have already mentioned several times, having the ability to edit fields directly in a list is a huge improvement and should gain us lots of increased productivity.

It should be noted upfront that you cannot directly change the issue type or the issue key from the **List** tool. To make a change to any value displayed on the screen, just click on the field, as illustrated in the following screenshot:

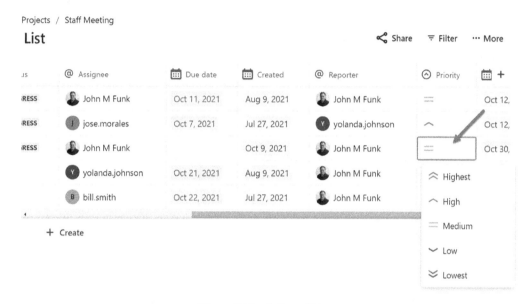

Figure 5.10 – Inline editing

Depending on the type of field, you will see an appropriate method to update the value. Clicking on a **Data type** field will immediately display a calendar function you can use to select a date. Clicking on a field with a list of values will provide a dropdown with available values (see *Figure 5.10* for an example of this). Clicking on user-related fields such as **Assignee** will display a list of users in your system who can be assigned to issues on this project.

Filtering issues

As with any listing of items, it is often desired to limit the actual issues that appear in the list. To do that, we need to apply an additional filter to the list received. Without any filters supplied, your JWM project list will include all issues on that project. To add a filter, click on the **Filter** icon at the top, as illustrated in the following screenshot:

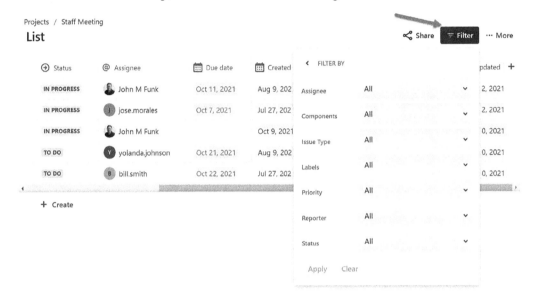

Figure 5.11 – Adding a filter to a list

As you click on the **Filter** icon, initially only the **Assigned to me**, **Due this week**, and **Done items** filters will appear. These are known as **Quick Filters** and provide a fast path to common filters. If you wish to search by additional fields, click on the **More Filters** option to see additional fields that can be used. Again, not all fields are currently available for searching/filtering.

See *Figure 5.11* for an example of adding other fields. Note that you can select multiple field options while in the **Filter** toolset. Each of these options will be cumulative, meaning that all of them will be used when you click the **Apply** button.

The filter icon will display the number of filters currently being used. If you want to return to the original list of **Quick Filters**, click on the back arrow to the left of **FILTER BY**.

Sorting issues

Finally, you can sort your list based on any column in your list. Clicking on the header will display an option to sort from **A – Z** or from **Z – A**, as illustrated in the following screenshot:

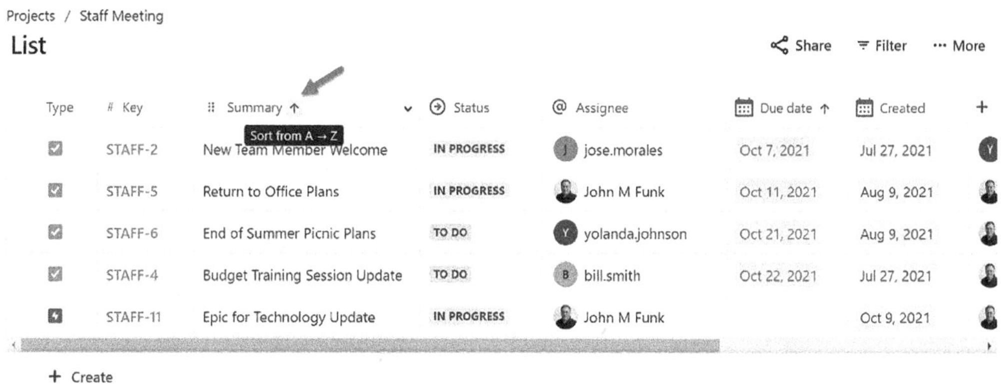

Figure 5.12 – Sorting a column

Though it is something of a misnomer, it will have these two options even when clicking on a date field. Just realize that it will sort the list based on either the most recent date for **A – Z** and the farthest away date for **Z – A**. Unlike filters, sorting is not currently cumulative. So, the most recent sort you have chosen will be the only sort used.

If you are using sub-tasks in your project, the **List** view will show the proper indentation of those tasks under their related parent task so you can quickly tell which issues are of the **Sub-task** type. Next, we will turn our attention to the **Timeline** feature.

Working with the Timeline

Roadmaps and **Gantt-style views** have long been missing from standard subscriptions in the Jira family of products. But in the last couple of years, Atlassian has made a concerted effort to bring this functionality to the masses.

First, we saw a simple roadmap appear with team-based software projects. Then came **Advanced Roadmaps**, which span multiple projects but are only available under a *Premium subscription*. And now, we see the equivalent in JWM projects under the name of **Timeline**.

Though it was the last of the features to come out with JWM, it has quickly gained traction and has much of the functionality you would expect with this type of tool. You can drag starting or ending points of issues to increase their length of time, you can add dependencies between issues, and—of course—you can export and share your timelines with others.

To access the **Timeline**, simply click on the **Timeline** menu option on the left, as illustrated in the following screenshot:

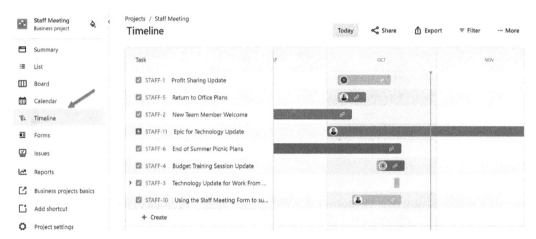

Figure 5.13 – The Timeline

Now, let's have a look at how to change durations.

Changing durations

As with any timeline or Gantt-style view, you will need to have start and end dates associated with your issue. JWM projects use the **Start date** field for the initiation of work on an issue and the **Due date** field for the end date when work should be completed.

To adjust the date ranges of your issue while in the **Timeline** view, click on the rectangular box associated with the issue at either the beginning (to change the start date) or the end of the box (to change the end date) and drag accordingly. Be sure to click on one of the slender handles that appear at the end of the box.

Alternatively, you can click on the **Issue** key to enter the full edit mode of the issue. There, you can change the **Start date** or **Due date** fields (or both). This will result in a graphical display of the issue to either lengthen or shorten, as illustrated in the following screenshot:

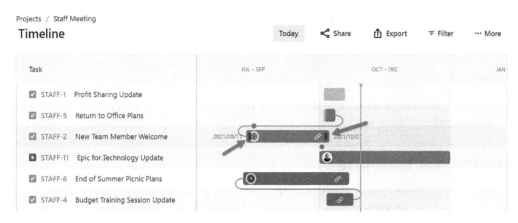

Figure 5.14 – Changing dates and durations

Dependencies

No timeline or roadmap would be complete without the ability to add dependencies between items of work. This is a simple procedure in JWM. Just click on one of the dots that appear at the ends of the issue as you hover over it, and then drag the dot on top of another issue.

The result will be a curved line connecting the end of one issue to the beginning of another issue, as illustrated in the following screenshot:

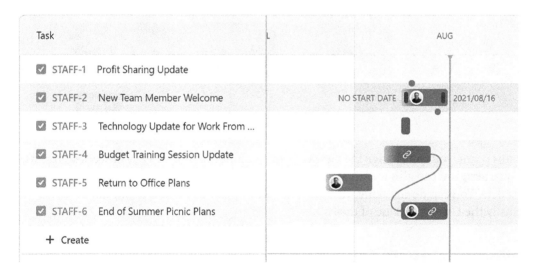

Figure 5.15 – Timeline dependencies

The timeline is intuitive enough to know which end you are dragging from to create the right type of dependency.

Timeline filters

Filters for timelines work exactly as they do for lists. See *Figure 5.11* and the surrounding descriptions of how filters work.

Exporting a timeline

It is often desirable to export timelines so that they can be added to presentations for stakeholder updates and general status inquiries. Simply click on the **Export** button to display the following screen:

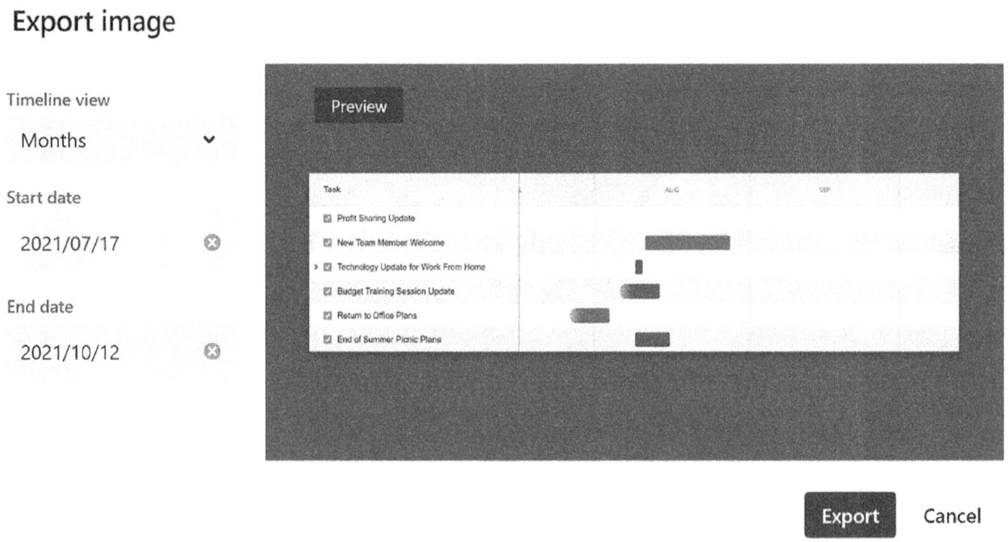

Figure 5.16 – Exporting a timeline

At this point, you can change the view of your timeline based on a view of weeks, months, or quarters. You can also identify the initial start date to exclude any issues starting before that date. You can do the same with the end date. Remember that the **End date** value is actually the **Due date** value of the issue.

Sharing a timeline

Outside of fully exporting a timeline, you can do a simple share of the **Uniform Resource Locator** (**URL**) for the timeline and send it directly to an existing Jira user, a Jira team, or an outside email address. Add a message if you like and click the **Send** button, as illustrated in the following screenshot:

Figure 5.17 – Sharing a timeline

The user will receive an email with a link to the timeline. Clicking the **Timeline** link in the email or the **View** button will take the user directly to your shared timeline.

For our final trip through the JWM features in this chapter, let's take a look at the **Calendar** feature.

Adding issues to the Calendar

Up until now, having a **Calendar** view of your project's issues required using a third-party Marketplace app or adding the **Calendar** gadget to a dashboard. Either way, you could not see the calendar from directly inside your project. The **Calendar** was one of the first features to be added to JWM and provided an immediate lift in functionality not found in other Jira products.

To date, the **Calendar** is still fairly simple, with little flexibility in how issues are displayed. But the simple fact that you can access it directly in the project makes it super helpful, and we expect the JWM development team at Atlassian to continue to produce new functionality. To display the calendar, click on the **Calendar** menu option on the left, as illustrated in the following screenshot:

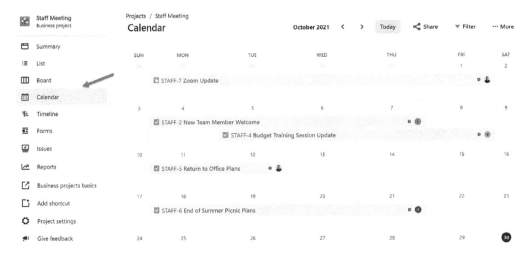

Figure 5.18 – The Calendar

The main driver to determine where on the calendar that issue will be displayed is the **Due date** field. The issue will appear on the calendar on the date associated with that field. If no filters are applied, you will see all issues in your project displayed on the calendar for any issues with a value in the **Due date** field. If the **Due date** field is not populated, the issue will not show on the calendar.

You can navigate to other months by clicking the left or right arrows adjacent to the name of the month and year. To return to the current month, simply click on the **Today** button. As with the previously explained filter functionality, see *Figure 5.11* and the surrounding descriptions to learn how to add filters.

Our last bit of functionality gives you the ability to create new issues directly from the calendar—the **Create issue** dialog box, as illustrated in the following screenshot:

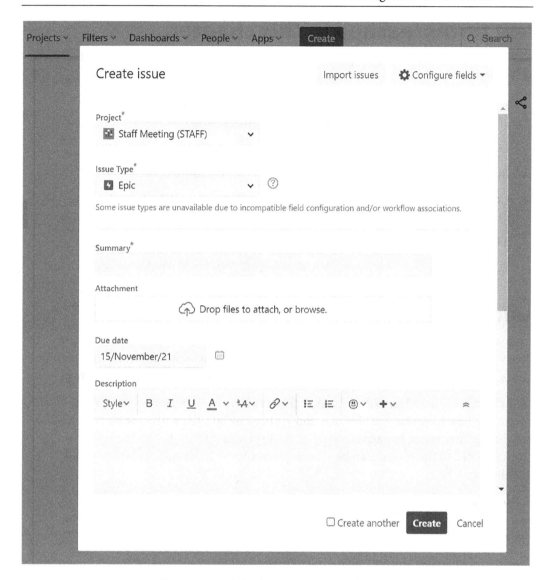

Figure 5.19 – Calendar: Create issue dialog box

To open the **Create issue** dialog box, double-click on one of the dates in the calendar. As the dialog box opens, it will automatically have the **Due date** field populated with the value of the date you double-clicked on.

New terms learned in this chapter

Let's conclude the chapter by going through the list of new terms learned in this chapter, as follows:

- **Summary**: The **Summary** section of a JWM project that shows statistics and activities that have been happening in your project.

- **List**: A list of all issues on your JWM project. It includes inline editing.

- **Board**: A Kanban-style view of your issues, presented as cards.

- **Calendar**: A calendar view of your issues, including interactive links allowing you direct access to the issue.

- **Timeline**: A roadmap or Gantt-style view of the issues in your project.

- **Forms**: A simple interactive screen allowing entry of fields when creating an issue.

Summary

I hope you are as excited as I am about the rebranding of Jira Core Cloud to JWM and the new features that are now available. Being able to not just view your issues in different formats but also interact with and make modifications to them is a real game-changer.

In this chapter, we have learned which new features have been deployed with JWM projects and how to access each feature, and we became familiar with how our items of work (issues) are related to each feature—their display and relationship. We saw how statistics related to the project can be seen as groupings of fields such as **Issue type** and **Priority**.

We also took the opportunity to do a deep dive into each component to further understand the functionality of each one and how to filter down issues when viewing each feature.

In the next chapter, we will continue exploring the features that come with JWM projects, including **Forms**. We will also learn how to create and run dashboards and reports and how to interact with issues in a more detailed manner.

6
Forms, Issues, Dashboards, and Reports

Our previous chapters have explored how to create **Jira Work Management** (JWM) projects and issues, which represent the work we do. We then looked at the new tools from JWM, how issues appear in each one, and the functionality they provide.

In this chapter, we will guide you through the creation of a simple JWM form, along with other reporting functions such as viewing issues, and working with dashboards, filters, and built-in system reports.

In this chapter, we are going to cover the following main topics:

- Creating forms
- Viewing issues
- Accessing and using reports
- Creating simple filters
- Implementing dashboards and incorporating gadgets
- New terms learned in this chapter

Upon completion of this chapter, you will be able to create a simple form that allows users inside or external to your team to be able to submit requests for work to be done. While the out-of-the-box reports provided with Jira offer little real insight, you will learn how to access and run the reports that are available.

Finally, you will be able to create ad hoc reports in the form of Jira filters and utilize filters to build informative dashboards. Then, you can view your issues in a variety of displays using the knowledge you have about filters.

Technical requirements

As JWM is only available in the Jira Cloud environment, the requirement for this chapter is simple: *access to a Jira Cloud environment.*

If you already have access to Jira Cloud, that's great—you are ready to go! If not, Atlassian provides a free JWM account for up to 10 users. You can create an account by going to `https://www.atlassian.com/try/cloud/signup?bundle=jira-core&edition=free` and following the instructions.

Creating forms

Until the rollout of JWM projects, there was no way to have organization-wide Jira project forms available without using a third-party vendor, which usually meant additional cost. There have been Atlassian Marketplace apps available for years, as well as portal forms for JSM, but this meant either additional license fees for JSM agents or purchasing an app from the vendor.

This will, of course, change as Atlassian begins to incorporate the **ProForma forms** functionality near the end of 2021 from the acquisition of ThinkTilt. It is unknown at the time of writing this book as to the effect of the ProForma tool across the Jira family, but it is thought that the built-in forms for JWM projects will continue alongside ProForma.

So, what's the big deal about using forms anyway? What advantages does a form provide that the normal **Create** button and its associated screen do not? The fast answer is that it can remove many pain points we experience with the typical request process on both the receiving and submitting ends of a request. Here is a quick list, with more details to follow in the subsequent highlighted section:

- Only ask for the initial information you need in an easy-to-fill format. (*Adding fields to a form*)

- Capture the information you want and eliminate back-and-forth emails. (*Adding fields to a form*)

- Change field labels to provide better context. (*Required fields and changing field labels*)

- An easy-to-share **Uniform Resource Locator** (**URL**) address for fast entry. (*Sharing a form*)

Now, let's look at how we get to the **Forms** feature and create a new form.

Creating a form

You can get to your form by clicking the **Forms** link on the left-hand menu, as illustrated in the following screenshot:

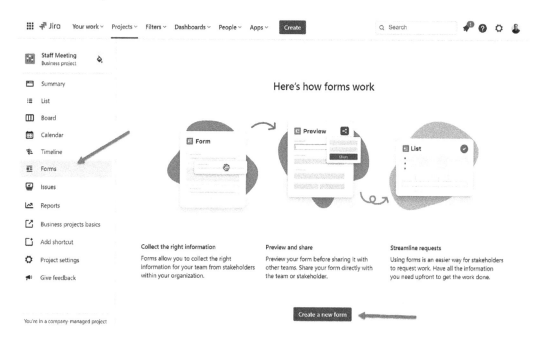

Figure 6.1 – Creating a form

You can then click on the **Create a new form** button to begin the process. Let's take a glance at the features of the form in the following screenshot, and then delve into the details in the subsequent paragraphs:

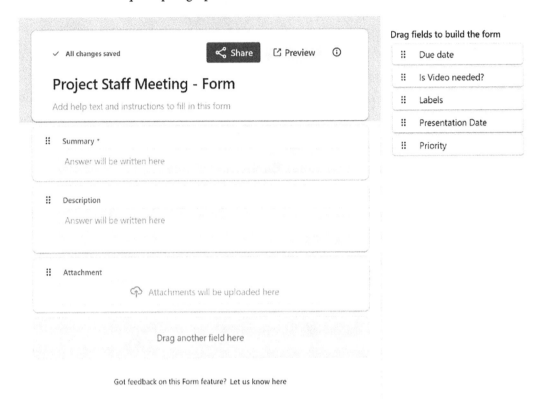

Figure 6.2 – New form

The large middle section is your actual form. It will contain a few default fields to get you started. Additional fields (including any custom fields you have created) are located on the right-hand side. The top-middle section contains the form name, description, and the ability to share the form.

Adding fields to a form

Nothing is more frustrating to a user than trying to figure out which fields really need to be populated when creating an issue. Screens are often awash with a sea of fields, most of which have nothing to do with the form creation process. Yes—you can provide the user with a separate **Create** screen with limited fields, but the layout can often be confusing.

Many helpdesks and request processes allow users to simply submit an email to an address. Subsequently, that results in an issue automatically being created on the appropriate project. However, the information submitted is usually lacking the depth and details needed for the receiver of the request to actually work on a solution.

The result is several emails back and forth to try to bring clarity by getting to the root of the problem. Not only is this impractical for the sheer number of emails that might happen, but the conversation becomes disjointed, and much time is wasted in the lag between sending and receiving the emails.

But with forms, you can identify the exact information you need captured upfront when a request is submitted. Simply add any custom fields you need for new information and drag the field to the left to build the form. Add your custom fields to the project, and they will show up on the right-hand side ready to be used. Then, it's a simple drag and drop, as seen in the following screenshot:

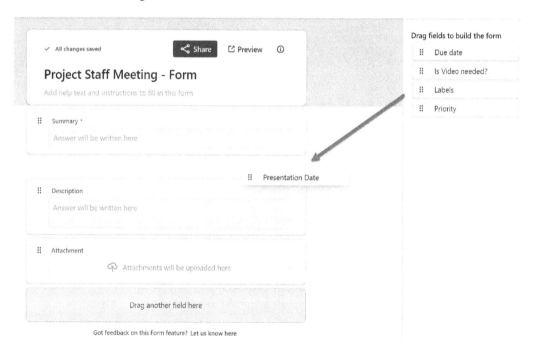

Figure 6.3 – Adding fields to a form

Once a field has been added to the form, you can drag the fields up and down to re-order the sequence in which they appear to the user. Of course, if you no longer want the field to appear on your form, simply drag the field back to the right-hand side under the **Drag fields to build the form** section.

Adding a description for a form

For clarity when sharing the form, it is a good idea to add a description to the form so that users can determine if this is the project and form desired. The description has wiki-style rendering available if you would like to make it look a little nicer. The following screenshot shows where you can enter a description:

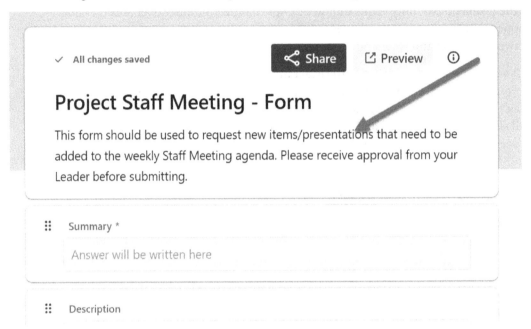

Figure 6.4 – Adding a form description

Next, we will see how required fields are identified and how to change labels for the fields.

Required fields and changing field labels

Having the ability to change the label of a field that users see makes the form clearer as to the intent of the desired value for the field. On normal **Create** screens, we are stuck with the label of the field being the actual field name. You cannot change that label without changing the actual field name in those cases. But with JWM forms, you simply click the pencil icon, which gives you access to edit the field, as illustrated in the following screenshot:

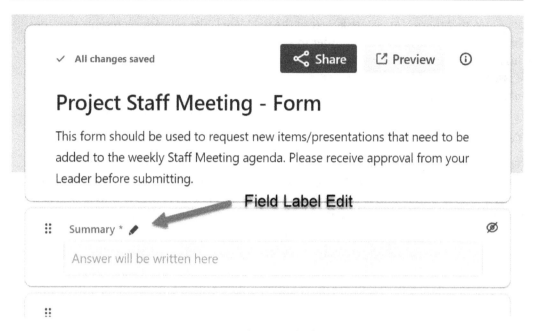

Figure 6.5 – Changing the field label

After making your label change, the field name will show your new name followed by the actual field name stored in the database. The field name will retain its original value; however, the requester will only see the new label. The label will be displayed above the entry box for the field, as shown in the following screenshot:

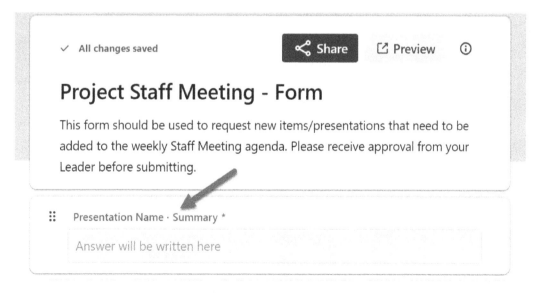

Figure 6.6 – Changed label name

Notice also that there is an asterisk next to the field label. The asterisk represents that the field is required to have a value in order to save and submit the request. You cannot make fields required directly in the JWM form—that must be done in the **Field Configuration** file associated with the project and issue type. You can find more details on field configurations in *Chapter 7, Managing Fields, Screens, and Issue Layouts*.

Previewing a form

After you have completed adding fields to your form and making any cosmetic changes such as changing label names or adding a description, it's time to preview your form. Of course, it is always a good idea to take a look at your form before sharing it with others. To see the form, click on the **Preview** button, as seen previously in *Figure 6.6*. Next, we see a preview of the created form, as illustrated in the following screenshot:

Figure 6.7 – Previewing a finished form

Clicking on the **Preview** button will cause the form to show up in a new tab in your browser while your form layout remains open in the original tab. You can continue to make changes to the form and then click the **Preview** button each time to see how it looks.

Sharing a form

Now that your form looks how it should, let's share it with others so that they can begin to use it. To do that, simply click on the **Share** button, which will open the dialog box shown in *Figure 6.8*. You can share a link to the form both with users in your Jira instance and external users to your system.

As you begin typing a name or email address, the names of users in your instance that match the characters you are typing will begin to show. You can select the names as they become visible. For an email address, continue to type the full address and then click on the result to be sure it is placed in the edit box, as illustrated here:

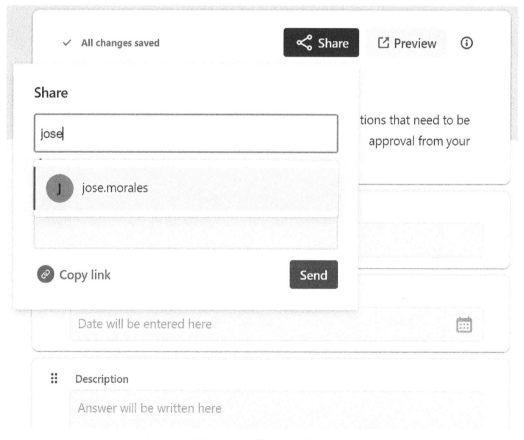

Figure 6.8 – Sharing a form

Your form is now ready to be used. Submissions will be added as issues on your project and will use the default issue type for the project if you have more than one standard issue type.

After the form is submitted, the user will receive an immediate notification on their screen that the issue has been received, as illustrated in the following screenshot:

We're on it!

Thanks for your submission. Want to also create forms and track your work with your team? Try Jira Work Management now.

Back to Jira

Figure 6.9 – Form submission

Now that users have an easy way to send you requests, let's look at some ways to interact with the issues.

Viewing issues

No matter how you receive issues—whether you create them directly yourself, or if they come via email or form submission—you will want to be able to view them and update them. If you receive an email notifying you that an issue has been created, clicking on the link in the email will take you directly to the issue.

However, you sometimes just need to take a look at a list of your current issues, or maybe even ones that have been completed in the past. While in your project, you are just a click away from this.

Regardless of which feature you might currently be viewing, you can click on the **Issues** menu option on the left to see your issues, as illustrated in the following screenshot:

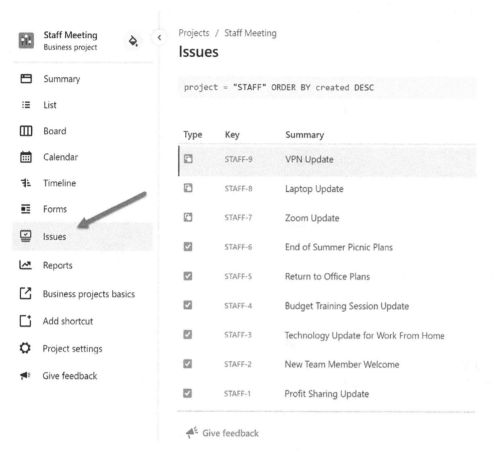

Figure 6.10 – Issues menu option

The **Issues** feature is a carryover tool from the previous Jira Core product. There's not been much of a change to it for those who have used it in the past, but for those of you who are new to the product now known as JWM, there are two standard views for issues—**List View** and **Detail View**.

List View is similar to the **List** tool discussed in *Chapter 5, JWM Toolset: Summary, List, Timeline, and the Calendar.* However, the view here allows no inline editing, but it does provide detailed search functionality for issues showing in the list. This can be done through a **Basic** filter interface or you can switch to **Jira Query Language** (JQL), Jira's built-in querying language.

List View was previously displayed in *Figure 6.10*, while **Detail View** can be seen in the following screenshot, which also shows where to click to switch between the two views:

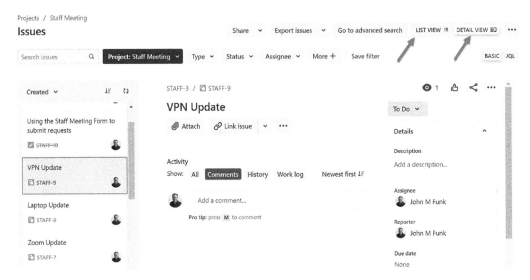

Figure 6.11 – Detail View with buttons to switch

Detail View allows you to edit a single issue using the project's **Edit** screen while also displaying the list of issues on the left-hand side. You can run a basic or advanced search on both **List View** and **Detail View**. Next, we will see how to access and run reports.

Accessing and using reports

Another holdover from the Jira Core product is the built-in Jira reports. These reports are not unique to JWM/business-type projects but are widely available across the Jira product family. Nevertheless, they can provide some informative insights into your project.

To access a list of reports, click on the **Reports** option on the left-hand side menu, as illustrated in the following screenshot:

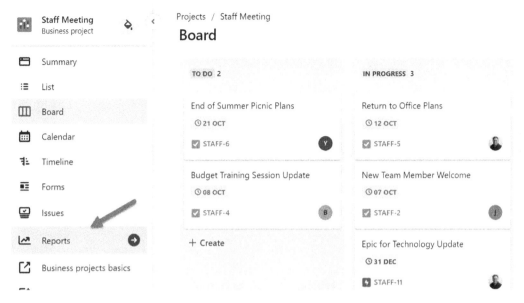

Figure 6.12 – Accessing reports

The result will be a display of all built-in reports available for JWM projects and is shown in the following screenshot. You are encouraged to explore each one individually:

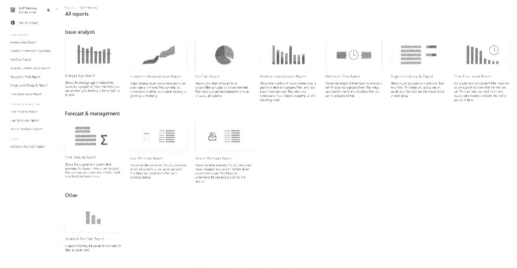

Figure 6.13 – List of reports

To run a report, just click on the link and follow the subsequent steps as directed. As you can imagine, there is not a lot of functionality for this basic reporting feature, and most users will end up creating ad hoc reports in the form of filters. Those filters can then be used in a variety of gadgets within dashboards or as filters themselves. We will explore all of those next.

Creating simple filters

Filters are Jira's way of searching for issues that exist in your instance that can be used as a base for further insight and reporting/sharing or to find a single issue that you are looking for. Perhaps the easiest way is to access these through **Issues View**, as discussed in the *Viewing issues* section earlier in this chapter. That will allow you to create a simple filter, which can then be used to see a list of issues immediately, or it can be saved and used as a base for building a dashboard.

Alternatively, you can click on the search box found in the top navigation menu. Once inside the search box, click on the **Advanced issue search** link, as illustrated in the following screenshot. Finally, you can also click on the **Filters** menu option at the bottom of the page:

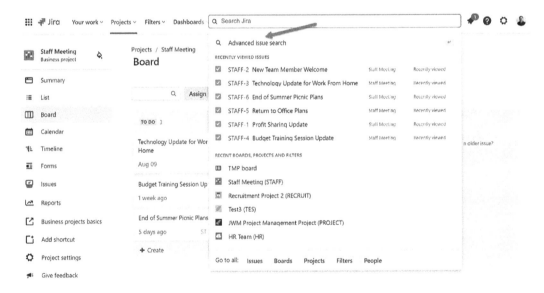

Figure 6.14 – Creating a filter

Even newcomers to Jira and JWM projects will be able to create simple filters to retrieve lists of issues that can be used for a variety of purposes, including gadgets in dashboards, for exporting to **comma-separated values (CSV)** files, or even just getting a count of how much work you are doing.

Entering the filter creation function in Jira will bring the user to the tool in basic mode, as shown in *Figure 6.15*. Simply click on each heading and supply the values you would like to use for the resulting list of issues, and then click on **Search**. There are many built-in fields already available to you to speed up the creation of a filter.

As you select each field, the filter builds upon itself, using an AND function between each field. This means that all of the values selected for every field will be used to return the results.

An initial filter to try is to select just the project you are working on and click the **Search** button, as illustrated here:

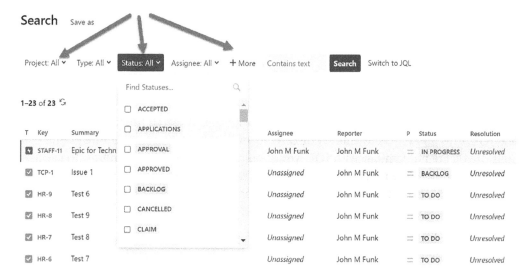

Figure 6.15 – Basic filter

You can also click on **Detail View** to see a single issue displayed, as we saw previously in *Figure 6.11*. In the following screenshot, we are filtering by **List View**:

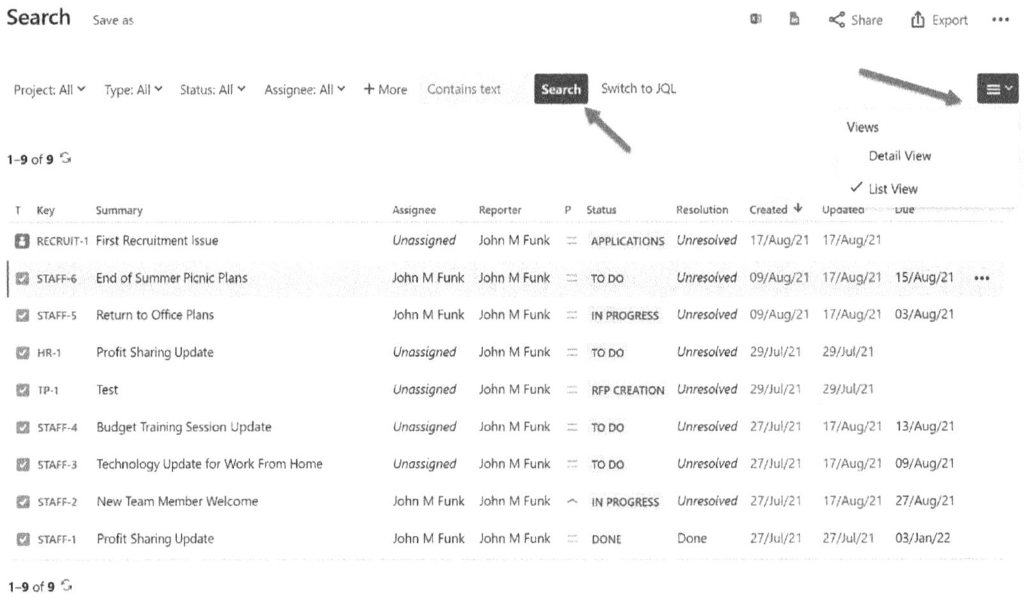

Figure 6.16 – Filtering by List View

For more experienced users, you can switch to the advanced search function directly using **JQL**. This allows you to enter code directly in the search box to see more granular results. If you are not familiar with JQL, you should take some training on how to use it before attempting to use it here. One such course is available through Atlassian University here: `https://university.atlassian.com/student/path/849533-gain-project-insights-through-jql`.

You can change back to the basic search function by clicking on the **Switch to basic** link to the right of the **Search** button, as illustrated in the following screenshot:

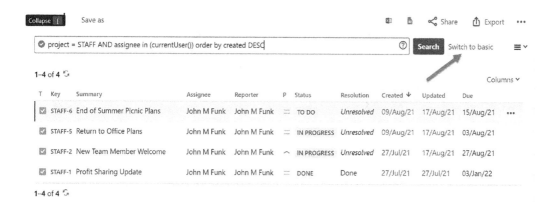

Figure 6.17 – Advanced JQL filter

More than likely, you are going to want to run these same filters repeatedly or use them in a dashboard gadget. Therefore, you will need to save the filter first. To start that process, click the **Save as** link at the top of the search display.

Saving a filter

Saving a filter is very simple. Just provide a unique name in the **Filter Name** box and click the **Submit** button. I have named mine STAFF – All Issues, as illustrated in the following screenshot:

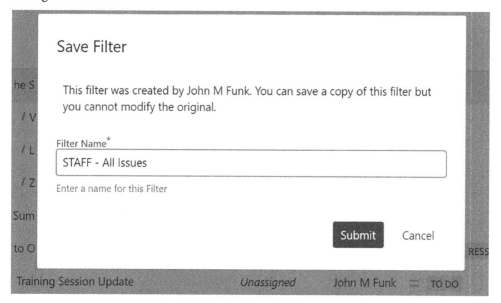

Figure 6.18 – Saving a filter

When you initially save a filter, you will be the only person able to see the results. You can leave it that way if you intend to keep the filter private, but if you want to share the filter and its results, you will need to modify the permissions. The place to do that is a little hidden. You will need to click on the **Details** link at the top of the filter screen, as illustrated in the following screenshot:

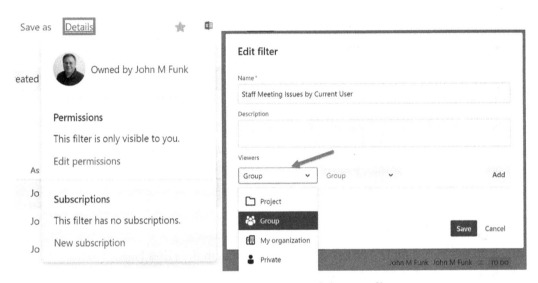

Figure 6.19 – Filter permissions and sharing a filter

After clicking on the **Details** link, you will navigate to the **Edit filter** screen. Incidentally, this is also where you will change the name of the filter if you wish to do that at some point. You can also add a description for the filter on this screen.

To share the filter, click on the drop-down box under the **Viewers** label. As you see in *Figure 6.19*, you can share the filter with persons linked to the **Project** through project roles, or to a **Group** of users already created in your Jira instance, or to your organization as a whole—meaning any logged-in user. If you wish to keep the filter to yourself, select the **Private** option.

Finally, you can create a **subscription** for the filter, which will email the filter and its results on a scheduled basis, as identified when creating it. To produce a subscription, click on the **New subscription** link on the **Details** page, as previously seen in *Figure 6.19*. Enter the details of the subscription and click the **Subscribe** button to save it, as illustrated in the following screenshot:

Filter Subscription

Recipients

Personal Subscription   ∨

Schedule

◉ Daily

◯ Days per Week

◯ Days per Month

◯ Advanced

Interval

once per day   ∨

at

11   ∨   00   ∨   pm   ∨

The timezone is the same as your profile's timezone - (GMT-06:00), Chicago

☐ Email this filter, even if there are no issues found

Subscribe   Cancel

Filter 6.20 – Creating a filter subscription

After you have created some filters, you can begin to use those filters in a variety of gadgets on a dashboard. Next, we will walk through the process of creating a dashboard and adding different types of gadgets.

Implementing dashboards and incorporating gadgets

Dashboards are a great way to see multiple reports on a single screen. Jira refers to these mini-reports as **gadgets**. Gadgets come in a variety of formats—bar graphs, pie charts, simple lists, and **two-dimensional (2D)** pivots. To create a new dashboard, click on the **Dashboards** option in the top navigation menu bar and select **Create dashboard**, as illustrated in the following screenshot:

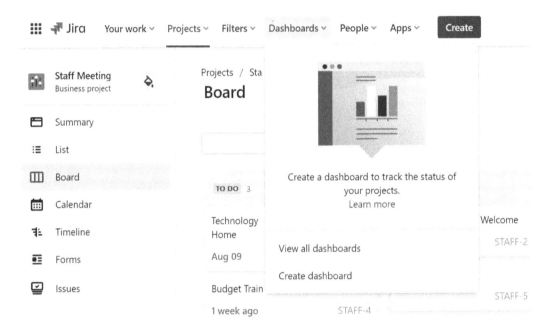

Figure 6.21 – Dashboards

The ensuing dialog box allows you to name the dashboard, along with entering a description. On this screen, you can also share the dashboard using the same permissions functionality we discussed earlier for filters (see *Figure 6.19)*. I have named mine Staff Meeting Dashboard, as illustrated in the following screenshot:

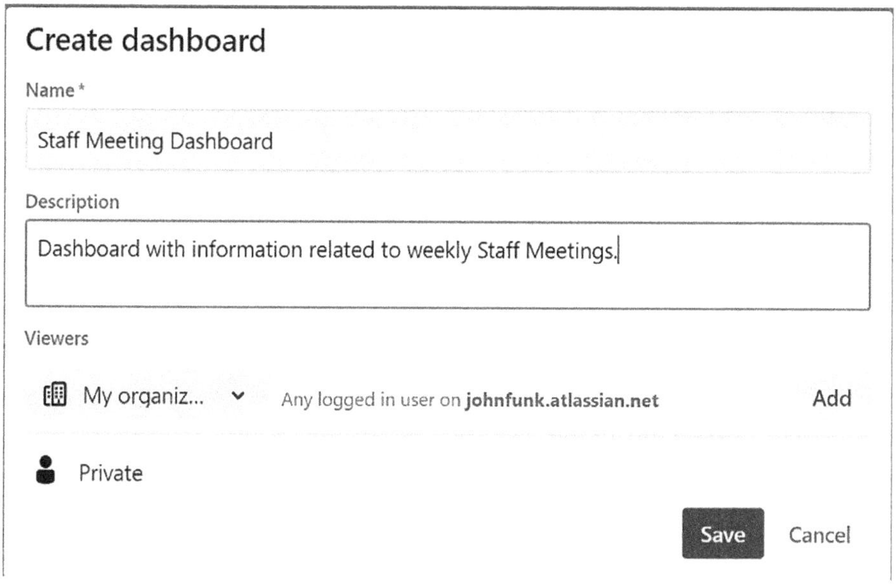

Create dashboard
Name *
Staff Meeting Dashboard
Description
Dashboard with information related to weekly Staff Meetings.
Viewers
My organiz...
Any logged in user on johnfunk.atlassian.net
Add
Private
Save
Cancel

Figure 6.22 – Naming and sharing a dashboard

After clicking the **Save** button, you will see the initially created dashboard. By default, the layout is a two-column dashboard. You can change the layout to a single column, triple columns, or dual columns, with either the right or left column being wider. Click the **Change layout** button to select your desired layout, as illustrated in the following screenshot:

Staff Meeting Dashboard
Add gadget
Change layout
Drag a gadget to this column or add a new gadget.
Drag a gadget to this column or add a new gadget.

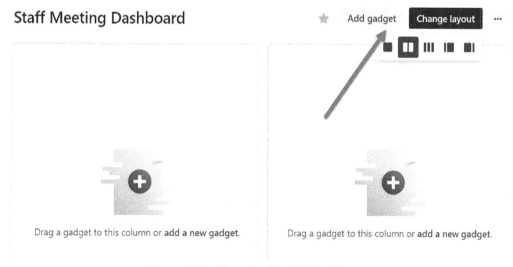

Figure 6.23 – Changing the dashboard layout

We will continue to use the two-column layout for our example here. Our next step will be to add some gadgets. So, click on the **add a new gadget** link on one of the sides of the screen. The initial list of gadgets will be very small. You will need to click the **Load all gadgets** option to see a more thorough list, as illustrated in the following screenshot:

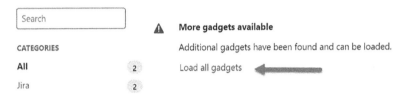

Figure 6.24 – Load all gadgets

The resulting list will show more than 30 options. Each will have a thumbnail image to the left to give you an idea of what the end report will look like. The name of the gadget and a short description appear in the middle section. Be sure to scroll down the alphabetical list to see all the available gadgets. Click on the **Add gadget** button on the right for each desired gadget.

The same list screen will continue to be displayed after you click on the **Add gadget** button. This enables you to select multiple gadgets without having to go back to the list for subsequent options. When you have finished selecting all your desired gadgets, click the **Close** button, as illustrated in the following screenshot:

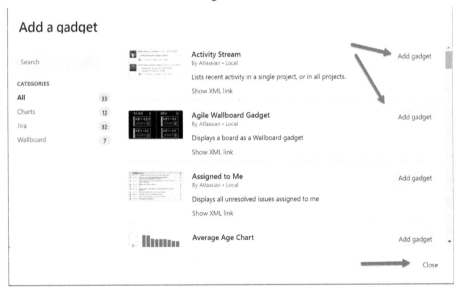

Figure 6.25 – Adding a gadget

Each gadget will have different parameters within the configuration page to capture the details of the filter, column headings, and so on. These should be self-explanatory as you complete the configuration.

Once the gadget has been added and the parameters have been entered, the results will be displayed (see the subsequently completed dashboard in *Figure 6.26*).

However, there is a good chance that you will need to modify the gadget to note additional information, change the filter, add new columns, and so on. To do that, click on the three dots (ellipsis) menu in the upper-right corner of the gadget and select **Configure**. This will return you to the configuration page for the gadget, as illustrated in the following screenshot:

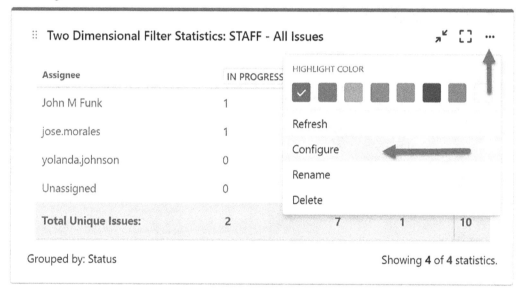

Figure 6.26 – Configuring a gadget

Once you are on the configuration page, you can change out the filter, the fields being used, and so on. Again, as each gadget is different, the configuration page for each is different. The following screenshot shows an example of a completed dashboard using three separate gadgets, which display a good variety available:

Figure 6.27 – Completed dashboard

I think you will find that a dashboard that is well laid out and has a good variety of gadget types that include a summary and detailed information will be a great way to share your project data with stakeholders and others.

New terms learned in this chapter

Let's conclude the chapter by going through a list of new terms learned in it, as follows:

- **Dashboard**: A consolidated display of multiple reports (known as gadgets).

- **Gadgets**: Usually based on filters, these mini-reports can be displayed as lists, graphs, charts, pivot tables, and so on.

- **ProForma forms**: An app or add-on that provides the extensive customization of standard forms.

- **Subscription**: Filter results that can be emailed to selected users on an ongoing basis.

Summary

Basically, at this point, you have all the knowledge you need to create a project and some issues and interact with them in a variety of ways to help manage your work. In this chapter, we have learned how to build a form, which will provide an easy way for persons inside or exterior to your team to make a work request. We have also seen how to use the **Issues** feature, along with the reporting function. This allows you to view your issues in a way that gives you good data and allows you to search with more control.

And finally, we learned how dashboards can provide you and stakeholders with easy-to-read gadgets that display your work in totals and groups or as easy-to-use graphics such as pie charts and bar graphs. These dashboards provide real-time views of your data, all in a single location. This is beneficial because you do not need additional presentation software or cut and paste efforts to transfer the Jira data to another format.

In the next chapter, we will learn how to create additional screens and custom fields for organization-wide use, and how to make modifications to those screens. This will be done in the context of understanding the associated screen scheme and issue-type screen scheme. And finally, we will see how we can change the layouts of the screens so that they can be unique to your project if so desired.

7
Managing Fields, Screens, and Issue Layouts

Our previous chapters explored how to create **Jira Work Management (JWM)** *projects* and *issues*, which represent the work we do. We then looked at the new tools in JWM, how issues appear in each tool, and the functionality these tools provide.

This chapter covers the creation and basic functions of *custom fields* and the types of fields that can be created. We will also explore what *screens* are automatically created when a new JWM project is created. And then, we'll see how to add custom fields to the screens.

We will discuss *issue layouts*, the different sections of the issue screen, and how to rearrange fields on a screen. This chapter also covers custom field contexts and how to limit the display of fields on screens based on the combination of projects and issue types.

In this chapter, we are going to cover the following main topics:

- Custom fields
- Using screens to view and edit your work
- How issue layouts affect the fields on your screens
- Screen schemes

By the end of this chapter, you will know how to create a new custom field, how to add the field to a screen in your project, and the basic functions of screens in JWM. You will also be able to modify the issue layouts of fields, for example, by moving fields between separate sections of a screen.

Finally, you will understand which schemes in the project are related to screens and which scheme type is linked to the project.

Technical requirements

As JWM is only available in the **Jira Cloud** environment, the technical requirement for this chapter is simple:

- Access to the Jira Cloud environment

If you already have access to Jira Cloud, that's great – you are ready to go! If not, **Atlassian** provides a free JWM account for up to 10 users. You can create your account by following the instructions at `https://www.atlassian.com/try/cloud/signup?bundle=jira-core&edition=free`.

Now, let's get started by looking at custom fields.

Creating and using custom fields

One of the most flexible options you can use when modifying your JWM projects is creating *custom fields*. There are several different field types available, but here are some of the most used:

- **Date picker**: This is used for dates only. It does not include time, although there is an additional field type that includes both date and time.
- **Number field**: This creates a simple number field that allows for decimals but not commas.
- **Radio buttons**: This creates a traditional radio button field where you supply the available options.

- **User picker (single user)**: This creates a dropdown for selecting a single licensed user in the system.

- **User picker (multiple users)**: This creates a field that allows for multiple users where you begin the selection by typing the initial letters of the user's name. Once selected, you can type and add additional usernames.

- **Paragraph**: This creates a paragraph-style field for entering text. It supports rich text rendering.

- **Short text**: This creates a regular text field for plain text only.

- **Select list (single choice)**: This creates a drop-down list of values that you supply.

- **Select list (multiple choices)**: This works like the multiple users user picker list, except you can provide the possible list of values. You can select multiple items in the list, but only one at a time.

- **Select list (cascading)**: This creates another type of select list where you provide the list values. However, a second field is available with values that depend on the values entered in the first field.

Next, let's see where we can access the custom fields.

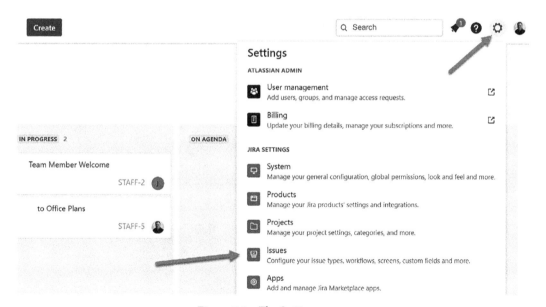

Figure 7.1 – The Settings menu

To create a new custom field or to modify an existing one, you will need to be a JWM administrator. To access the custom fields function, follow these steps:

1. Select the gear icon to open the **Settings** menu on the far-right side of the top navigation bar.

2. Then, choose the **Issues** option.

3. Finally, click **Custom fields**.

After arriving on the next screen, click **Custom fields** on the left-hand side menu, as shown in *Figure 7.2*:

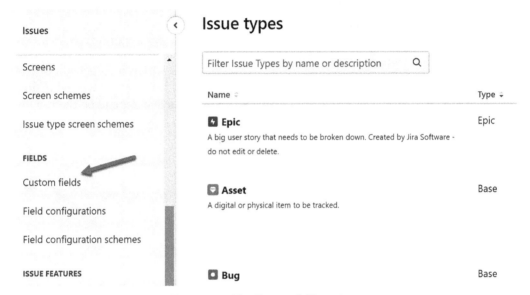

Figure 7.2 – The Custom fields option

Clicking **Custom fields** will open a screen displaying a list of all the current custom fields in your instance. You can use the search box to find a specific custom field or to verify if a field by that name already exists.

To create a new custom field, click on the **Create custom field** button on the top-right of the screen:

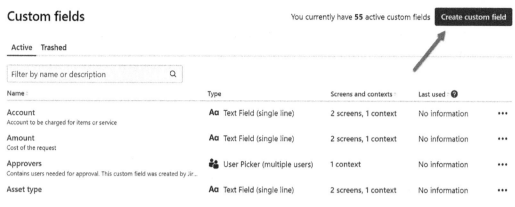

Figure 7.3 – Creating a custom field

At this point, you will see a list of the available field types. Notice that on the left-hand side, the default is for the standard list of field types. You can also click on **All** or **Advanced** to see additional field types.

For our example, we are going to choose the date picker field type by clicking **Date Picker**. Once selected, click the **Next** button to continue to the next step:

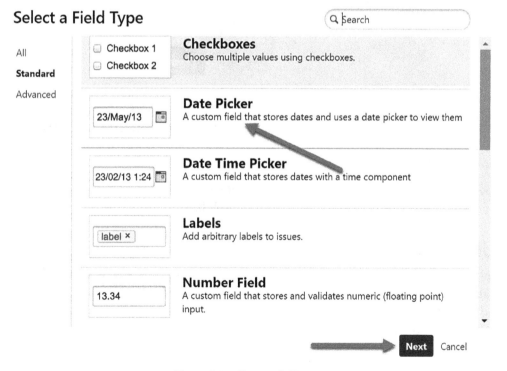

Figure 7.4 – Custom field types

> **Note**
> Once you create a custom field, you cannot change or convert its type. If you incorrectly choose the wrong field type when you create the field, or if you change your mind as to the preferred type, you will need to create a new field.

Although it might seem out of sequence, you choose the field type before entering the name of the field. *Figure 7.5* displays the **Name** and **Description** fields that allow you to add these values for the custom field:

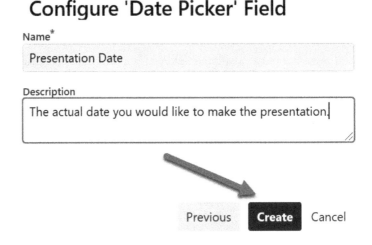

Figure 7.5 – Naming a custom field

For our example, we have chosen to name the field `Presentation Date`. After you have selected your field type and added a name for your custom field, click the **Create** button (as seen in *Figure 7.5*). Your new custom field is now created!

However, the new field will not be visible on any screens yet. So, the next display after your field is created will allow you to immediately add the field to an existing screen(s).

Adding fields to screens

To add your field to ALL screens in your instance, you can click on the box to the right of the **Tab** heading, as highlighted by the arrow on the right-hand side in *Figure 7.6*. This is a handy way to add the field to multiple screens without having to click every box. You may eventually have dozens or even hundreds of screens, so this is a quick method to use:

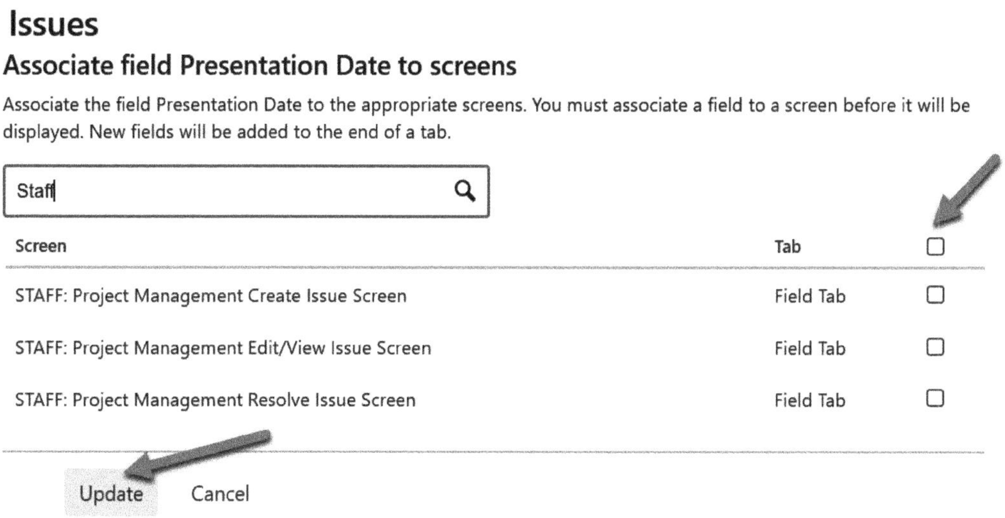

Issues

Associate field Presentation Date to screens

Associate the field Presentation Date to the appropriate screens. You must associate a field to a screen before it will be displayed. New fields will be added to the end of a tab.

Staff	Q

Screen	Tab	☐
STAFF: Project Management Create Issue Screen	Field Tab	☐
STAFF: Project Management Edit/View Issue Screen	Field Tab	☐
STAFF: Project Management Resolve Issue Screen	Field Tab	☐

Update   Cancel

Figure 7.6 – Adding a custom field to a screen

Of course, you might want to add the field to only a single screen or a handful of screens. To do that, enter some text in the search box for the screen(s) you would like to narrow the **Screen** list to. In our example, we have typed in Staff. As you type the letters, the list will immediately filter down to screens matching your search.

Then, select the checkbox for each desired screen and click the **Update** button. At this point, the custom field has been created and is available for use on all of the screens you selected. For our example, we are entering the word Staff for our project and linking the custom field to the STAFF project screens.

Note

You may be tempted to create a new custom field for every need you have for every screen in every project. However, an excessive number of custom fields will slow your system down. Because of this, creating new custom fields should be done sparingly.

Let's take a look at how we can limit the impact of custom fields on our system and how they can clarify the intended values to be entered.

Editing the context for a custom field

Of course, once a custom field has been created and linked to a screen, you might need to edit information about the field. However, one of the first things you will want to do is to edit the *context* associated with the field.

To edit the context of the field, we return to the list of custom fields (as shown in *Figure 7.2*). Enter some text in the search box to find your new field. Again, we will use the `Presentation Date` field for our example.

When you have displayed the desired field, click the ellipsis menu (**...**) on the right-hand side of the field row and select **Contexts and default value**:

Figure 7.7 – Configuring a custom field

The resulting screen will display various sections, including a list of *issue* types and *projects*.

The *context* will link the field to the project(s) and/or issue type(s). Connecting the field to at least one project or at least one issue type will help tremendously with any system resource issues related to custom fields. Fields that are global for both projects and issue types are taxing to the system and may result in errors and slow performance:

Choose applicable issue types

Please select the applicable issue types. This will enable the custom field for these issues types in the context specified below.

Apply for all issues with any selected issue types

Choose applicable context

Please choose the contexts where this configuration will be applicable. Note that this will apply to only issues with the selected issue type as above.

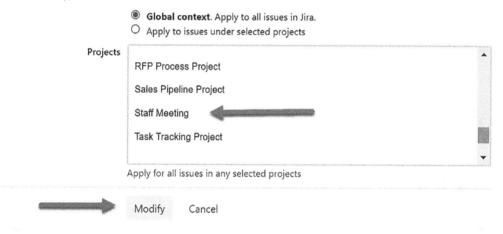

Figure 7.8 – Updating the field context

To select an issue type or project, simply search for its name in the appropriate section and click it. If you want to select multiple values in that section, be sure to hold down the *Ctrl* (PC) or *Command* (Mac) key when clicking on the second and subsequent values.

Finally, click the **Modify** button to save the changes to the context. If you want to switch back to not having a value selected, you can click the **Any issue type** value under **Issue types** or the **Global context** radio button in the **Projects** section.

To change the name of the custom field, return to the list of fields and select **Edit details** from the ellipsis (**…**) menu. Then, simply change the name. Be aware that changing the name of the field might cause automation rules or workflow post functions to fail:

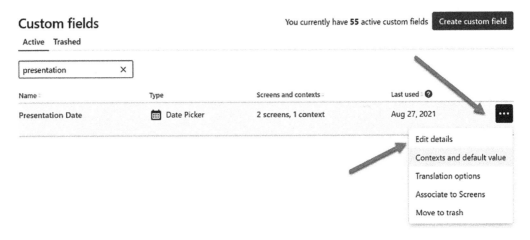

Figure 7.9 – Changing the name of a custom field

Next, we will learn how to arrange our new custom fields on project screens.

Using screens to view and edit your work

During the custom field creation process, you can choose screens (or none) to contain your field. However, when you select a screen(s) for your field, the field is simply placed at the bottom of the list of fields for that screen. Perhaps you would like to move the field to a different position on the screen. Or maybe you chose not to link the field to any screen during the creation process.

Either way, let's explore how we can make these modifications once the custom field has been created. To access the screens, go to **Settings | Issues | Screens**. This leads to the screen shown in *Figure 7.10*:

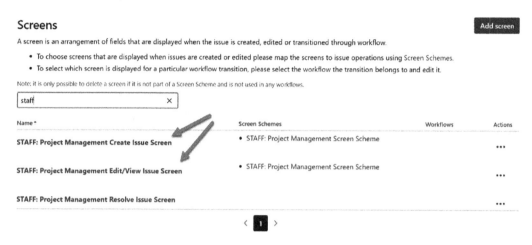

Figure 7.10 – Identifying screens

Simply type some text in the search box for the screen you are looking for and any screens matching the text will automatically appear. It is important to recognize that there might be different screens available for our project.

For most JWM projects, two default screens will be created for the project: the **Create Issue Screen** and the **Edit/View Issue Screen**. An additional **Resolve Issue Screen** might be created for selected projects. The reason for the difference in the two default screens is that you may want fewer fields or different fields available when creating a new issue versus when editing an existing issue. Having fewer fields usually provides clarity and simpler input values for the person creating the issue.

To edit which fields are shown on the screen or to rearrange their order, just click on the screen name. At this point, the **Configure Screen** window will appear:

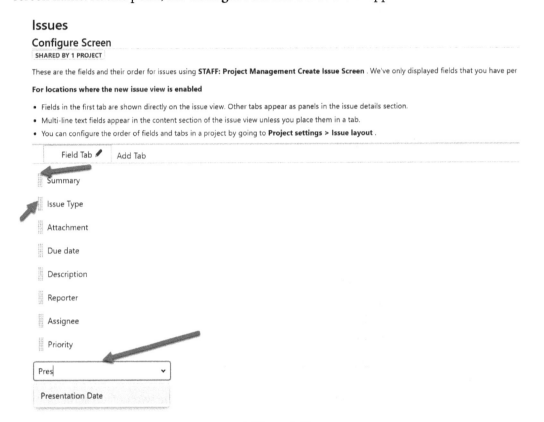

Figure 7.11 – Adding a field to a screen

To add a field, simply start typing the name of the field and values will begin to be shown. For our example, we are adding the `Presentation Date` field that we previously created. When the value appears, click on the field name. To rearrange the order in which the fields appear, click on the left-hand side handle and drag the field up or down.

Next, we will take a look at the sections of a screen and how to move fields to different areas on screens. *Figure 7.12* displays the various sections of a screen, and this is followed by a short description of each:

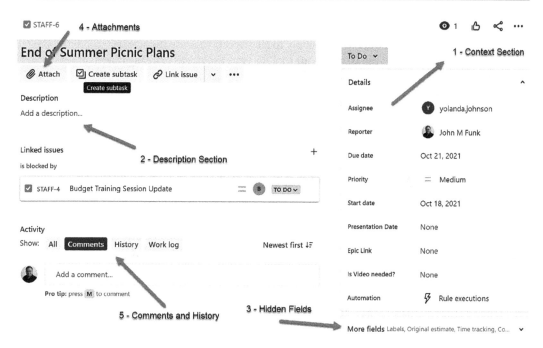

Figure 7.12 – Editing fields on a screen

Let's take a look at each section of the screen:

1. **Context section**: By default, this contains all non-paragraph/multi-line text fields. This includes the following field types: number, date, user picker, select list, and single-line text.

2. **Description section**: By default, this contains only paragraph or multi-line text fields and the **Summary** field.

3. **Hidden fields**: This contains fields that are hidden if they contain no value. Clicking the **More fields** link will display or hide the fields.

4. **Attachments**: The **Attach** button must appear on the screen if you want to be able to add attachments to the issue. This section also contains the **Create subtask** and **Link issue** buttons.

5. **Comments and history**: The **Activity** section contains a wealth of information. Clicking the **Comments** tab shows all comments that have been added to the issue. The **History** tab will show all changes that have taken place with the issue since it was created. The **Work log** tab shows any time that has been recorded/charged to the issue.

Though the attachments and activity sections are not actually sections for adding or moving fields, they show information related to the fields for the issue.

> **Note**
>
> The order of fields on a screen will apply to all projects that use the screen. However, you can use the **Issue layout** tool for your project to rearrange the fields for just that project, without affecting other projects.

Now that we know how to create custom fields and add them to a screen, next, we will see how we can move the fields between sections on the screen for the related project.

How issue layouts affect the fields on your screens

To modify the layout of the fields used by the screen for your project only, click on the **Issue layout** link on the left-hand side menu when in the **Project settings** screen. You must be a project administrator to access the project settings and modify the issue layout:

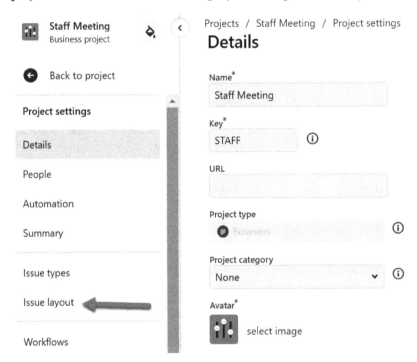

Figure 7.13 – The Issue layout link in the Project settings window

After selecting this option, you will advance to the **Issue layout** screen, as seen in *Figure 7.14*. If you have multiple screens for different issue types in your project, you will be able to edit the layout of each screen. See *Figure 7.16*, which is toward the end of this chapter, for more details on issue type screen schemes:

Figure 7.14 – Editing the issue layout

To modify the location of the fields on your screen, simply click on the **Edit layout** link on the right-hand side of the **Issue layout** screen (*Figure 7.14*).

On the **Issue layout** screen, you can drag fields from section to section. *Figure 7.15* highlights these sections, which we will list in detail next:

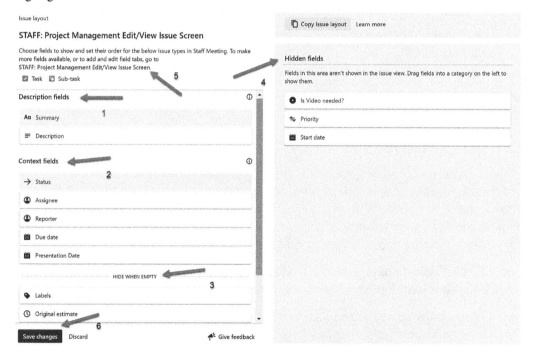

Figure 7.15 – The sections of the Issue layout screen

Let's look at each of these in detail:

1. **Description fields**: This relates to the **Description** section, previously seen in *Figure 7.12*. Although this originally contained multi-line text fields, you can drag other types of fields into this section, except for the **Status** field.

2. **Context fields**: This relates to the **Context** section, previously seen in *Figure 7.12*. You can drag other types of fields into this section, including the **Description fields**. However, you may not move the **Summary** field into this section.

3. **HIDE WHEN EMPTY**: This relates to the **Hidden Fields** section, previously seen in *Figure 7.12*. Fields in this section will not show on the screen if the field has no value.

4. **Hidden fields**: Fields in this section will not show on the screen at all for this project.

5. **Screen name**: Click on this link if you want to edit the base screen used by the issue layout.

6. **Save changes**: When all of your changes are complete, be sure to click the **Save changes** button.

In our final section, we will see how screens can be grouped into *schemes* for attachment to a project.

Screen schemes

We began the process of adding screens to our project by simply creating the screen. However, the screen cannot be directly attached to the project to begin using it. First, it must be added to a screen scheme. As we saw in *Chapter 4*, *Modifying the Board, Workflow, and Associated Schemes*, a *scheme* can be thought of as a bucket holding various items. Therefore, a *screen scheme* would be a scheme consisting of multiple screens.

So, our **STAFF: Project Management** screen scheme contains the **Create Issue Screen** and the **Edit/View Issue Screen**, as we saw in *Figure 7.10*.

Figure 7.16 shows the related screen components accessed from the **Settings | Issues path**. Because multiple issue types can be connected to a project and because each issue type can have a separate screen scheme associated with it, these are all connected in a second scheme called the *issue type screen scheme*.

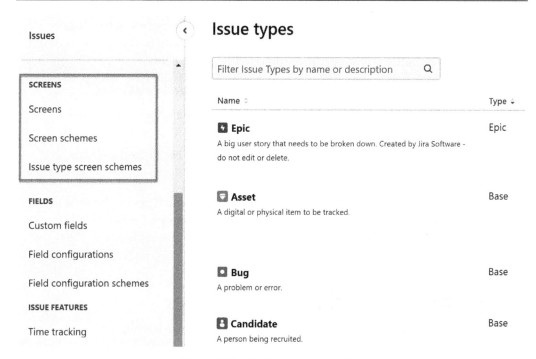

Figure 7.16 – The Issue types window

This scheme is then attached to the project, as opposed to the individual screens themselves. *Figure 7.17* shows the relationship between the screens and related schemes:

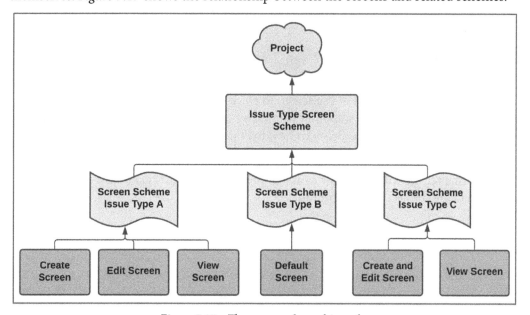

Figure 7.17 – The screen scheme hierarchy

When you create the JWM project, these screens and screen schemes are automatically created and related to each other. Let's talk about this structure briefly. If you were to build these connections from the ground up, you would follow this process:

1. Create your base screen and populate the screen with your desired fields.

2. Create a screen scheme – this scheme will be based on the screen you created in *Step 1*.

3. Create an issue type screen scheme – this scheme will be based on the screen scheme you created in *Step 2*.

Another description of the relationship between screens and issue types can be seen in the Atlassian documentation at `https://bit.ly/3BBuzCq`. Though the notation is for Atlassian **Data Center** and **Server**, the graphics and descriptions are still relevant for **Jira Cloud**.

New terms learned in this chapter

Let's conclude the chapter by going through a list of new terms we learned:

*   **Custom fields**: These are fields of various types such as text, number, pick lists, and user lists, which are created and assigned to a *context*. The fields can appear on multiple screens.

*   **Context**: These link fields to projects and/or issue types.

Summary

In this chapter, we learned how to create new custom fields, attach them to an existing screen, and configure the layout of the screen to place the fields in the appropriate sections. All of this allows for a smoother user experience, as fields can appear in a context that makes more sense. We have also seen how to configure our custom fields so that they are not a drain on system resources by linking each to a project and/or issue type.

In the next chapter, we will learn how to assign permissions to users and how to carry out simple system and project administration.

Section 3: Administering Jira Work Management Projects

Upon completion of this section, you will be able to carry out basic and advanced administration of **Jira Work Management** (**JWM**) projects. You will also have learned how to extend JWM functionality using automation and creative project creation.

This section contains the following chapters:

- *Chapter 8, Configuring Permissions and Simple Administration*
- *Chapter 9, Duplicating Projects and Starting outside of the Box*
- *Chapter 10, Using Project Automation*

8
Configuring Permissions and Simple Administration

Now that we have our project up and running and have added new custom fields to provide more insight into our issues, we need to be able to share access to the project and the issues. This will include creating or inviting new users and placing them in the appropriate groups. You can then assign project permissions to the user based on their user account or the group in which they reside.

This chapter covers the nuances of configuring permissions for both free and paid accounts and how to apply additional security within the project. Then, we will cap it off with a brief discussion of some simple project administration functions that we have not learned yet.

Jira Work Management approaches permissions and access to the information differently based on whether your account is a free account or a paid one. Also, we will see some slight differences in simple project administration based on free and paid accounts and what is available to manage at the higher system or global level for Jira.

In this chapter, we are going to cover the following main topics:

- Adding users and creating groups
- Project roles and permission
- Configuring the permission scheme
- Applying issue-level security
- JWM project administrator capabilities
- Jira administrators versus project administrators

By the completion of this chapter, you will learn how to invite new users and add project roles and users to the roles. Once those are in place, you will be able to access and modify the **Permission Scheme** to use those roles and users, and then learn how to create and apply issue security levels.

To be able to manage your project more fully, you will learn the capabilities available to project administrators and the differences between Jira administrator and project administrator permissions.

Technical requirements

As Jira Work Management is only available in the Jira Cloud environment, the requirement for this chapter is simple: *access to a Jira Cloud environment.*

Atlassian provides a free Jira Work Management account for up to 10 users. You can create your account by going to `https://www.atlassian.com/try/cloud/signup?bundle=jira-core&edition=free` and following the instructions.

User management

When you first set up a new instance/site for Jira – in this case, a new instance of Jira Work Management – the email address used during the signup will create a user that is a Jira administrator, an organization administrator, and a site administrator. A very brief description of each follows:

- **Jira administrator**: The Jira Administrator can make all changes at the system and project level within your Jira instance for the products the user has been granted access to. These are often referred to as **global permissions**. However, they cannot grant access to users to join your instance.

- **Organization administrator**: When you create a new instance/site, an organization is automatically created as well. Initially, it will be named the same as your site. The organization administrator will be able to add other organization administrators, create system-level **API keys**, verify **domains** for your site, implement **Atlassian Access**, and control the **directory** of managed users for your domain.

- **Site administrator**: The site administrator can grant users access to products in your instance by inviting them to the instance. Consequently, they can also deactivate user access to the products. They can also create **groups** and assign users to those groups.

To access the user management function of Jira, you must be a site administrator. You can only become a site administrator by being granted that permission by another site administrator. To make a user a site administrator, you simply place that user in the **site-admin** group under **User management**.

To gain access to the user management function, click on the **Settings** gear icon in the top navigation bar and select **User management**, as shown in *Figure 8.1*:

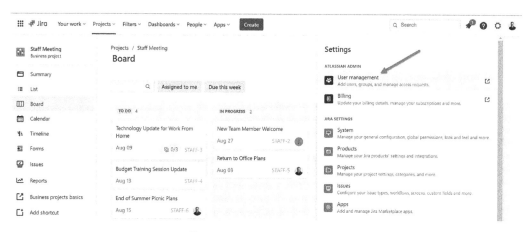

Figure 8.1 – User management

The result will bring you to a list of current users at the bottom of the screen and a section at the top of the screen where you can invite new users. As seen in *Figure 8.2*, there are two different ways to initially invite a user.

One option is to simply begin adding the email addresses of the invitees in the center section of the display with one email address per box. The invitees will get an email that will be needed to verify the account and accept the invitation. You cannot create accounts for users without the email being validated by the recipient of the email address. To send the emails, click on the **Invite team members** button at the bottom of the section:

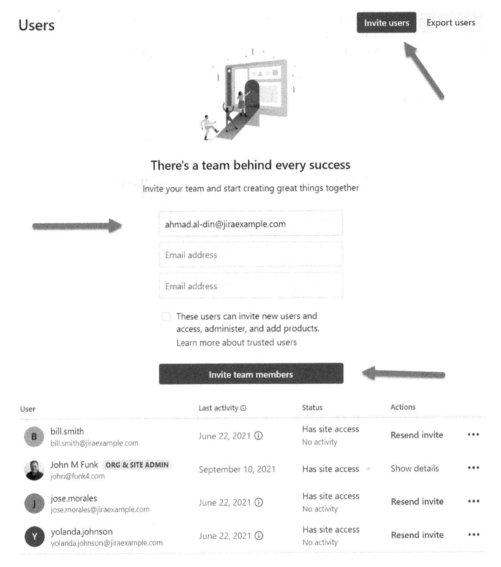

Figure 8.2 – Invite users

The second way to invite users begins by clicking on the **Invite users** button at the top of the screen. This will open the dialog box seen in *Figure 8.3*.

This option gives you more flexibility as to which groups and permissions you can automatically assign to the user when the invitation is accepted. Just enter the email address of the future user, choose the role and products the user can access, and include any groups.

You can pick from one of three roles. The following descriptions will be displayed for each role on the screen:

- **Basic**: Can access the products you specify only
- **Trusted**: Can update product settings, add new products, and invite basic users to products
- **Site Administrator**: Can administer your site, determine user access, and update billing details (like you)

Figure 8.3 shows how to invite new users to your instance. You can invite one user or multiple ones:

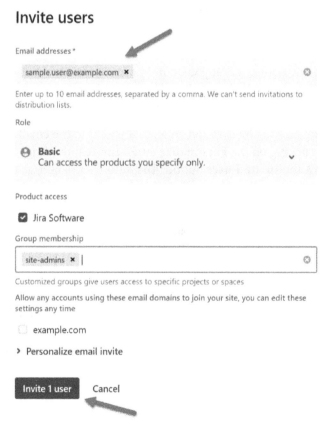

Figure 8.3 – User information

If you have not created any additional groups yet (we will do that later in this section), your initial options for adding groups will be:

- **jira-software-users**: This is the most basic level of access needed to perform functions in Jira Work Management. Users will have no product access without being in this group.

- **jira-administrators**: This grants the user the ability to administer the features within your Jira instance, such as screens, custom fields, issue types, and workflows.

- **site-admins**: As mentioned above, this grants the user the ability to add/remove other users and create groups and maintain their memberships.

- **Administrators**: This is basically a combination of the jira-administrators and site-admins roles, giving the user full access to the system. This is sometimes referred to as a *super user*.

Once you have added an email address (or more), a statement will appear, as shown previously in *Figure 8.3*, that states, **Allow any accounts using these email domains to join your site, you can edit these settings any time**. It will then list each domain from the email addresses listed in the top box.

You should not select any domains that you do not have control over, for example, gmail. com. Clicking on one of the email domain boxes will allow any person with an email address under that domain to gain access to the system without needing an invite first.

Finally, you can personalize the invitational email that is sent to the email address(es) entered at the top by clicking on the **Personalize email invite** link. When you are ready to send the email, click the **Invite 1 user** button. The number will change based on the number of emails entered above.

Once you have invited users, they will be added as users in your system. The new users will show up at the bottom of the screen, as shown previously in *Figure 8.2*. A screenshot of that bottom section is shown in *Figure 8.4*.

User list

The list of users has some excellent information, including the **Last activity** date of the user (basically meaning the last time the user logged in), the **Status** of the user (or whether the user is active or inactive), and finally, under **Actions**, whether the user has accepted the invite:

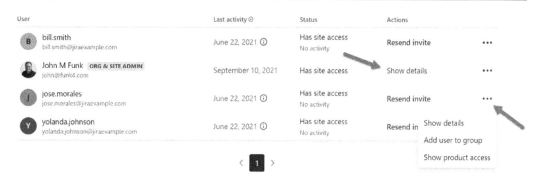

Figure 8.4 – User list

Also, you can click on **Show details** for active users to see more personal information, such as what groups each user belongs to and their current role in the system (the same **Role** shown in *Figure 8.3*). You can add users to a group on that user detail page, or you can click on the ellipsis menu (three dots) and add at that point.

Next, we will follow the process to create new groups. While on the left-hand menu, click **Groups**:

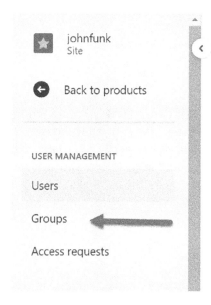

Figure 8.5 – Groups

The result will land you on the **Groups** page, showing a list of all current groups in your system. Again, when you first set up your Jira instance, there will be just a handful of groups created with the system. To add a new group, click on the **Create group** button in the top right of the screen:

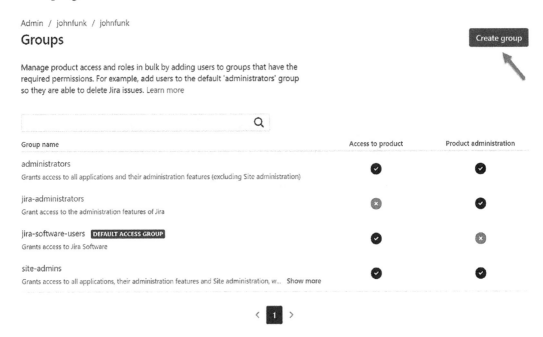

Figure 8.6 – Create group

As you arrive on the screen displayed in *Figure 8.7*, you will have the ability to enter the **Group's name** (required) and the **Group's description**, if so desired. For our example, we will create a group called Staff Meeting Access, which we will later use for issue-level security. This group will represent the users who will have access to all issues on the staff meeting project:

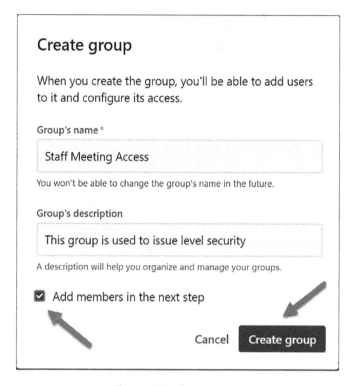

Figure 8.7 – Group name

You can check the box for **Add members in the next step** to associate users with the group or you can return to the group later to add the names. When ready, click the **Create group** button to finalize your group. Next, we will discuss project roles and permissions.

> **Important Note**
>
> Currently, you cannot change the name of the group once it is created, so be thoughtful when adding the group name. This bug is on Atlassian's list to fix in the future.

Project roles and permissions

As with any system, you need some basic authentication and permission capability for the first level of security of your information. Jira Cloud provides you with authentication of users when you create your initial instance of Jira/Jira Work Management. Authentication is simply the process of validating that a user is who they really are when they log into the system.

As your organization grows, you can extend this capability using the Atlassian Access tool to provide more control of the user setup and authentication process. See `https://www.atlassian.com/software/access` for more information.

There are two ways to control access to your project, both of which involve the **permission scheme**. One route would be to handle all the permissions directly in the permission scheme by granting permissions directly to individual users or groups.

But this is the least advised method, as it hampers the sharing of the scheme with projects that have different users. If you modify the permission scheme to use project roles instead, that gives you more flexibility with sharing the scheme. Let's look at that second option now:

1. To modify who is linked to roles on your project, you must be a project administrator.

2. Next, you will click on **Project settings**, as shown in *Figure 8.8*:

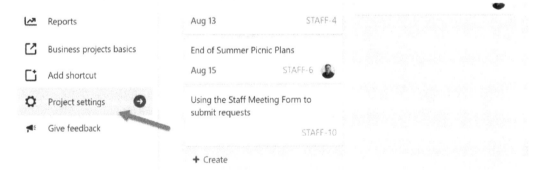

Figure 8.8 – Project settings

3. As you enter **Project settings**, select the **People** option. If you are on a **free** plan, you will not be able to modify permissions or change the role assignment of persons on any of your projects:

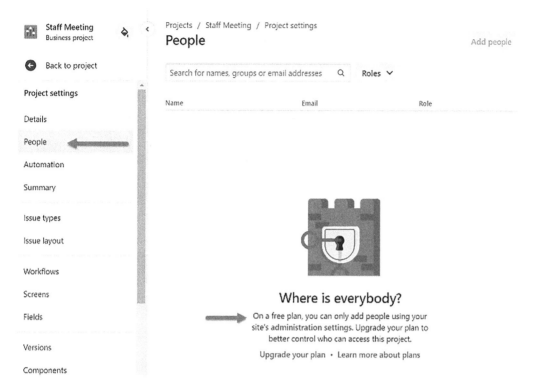

Figure 8.9 – People – free plan

4. If you are on a **paid** plan of any level, you will be able to adjust permissions across your instance, including for all projects. As you enter the **People** screen, you will see a list of all groups and/or individual users who have access to the project and the project roles to which they are attached:

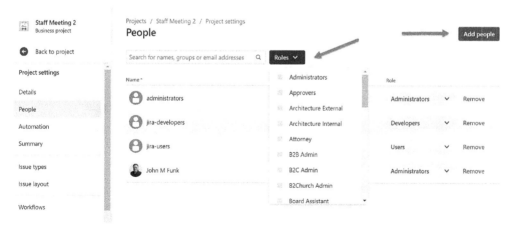

Figure 8.10 – People – paid plan and roles

5. Click on the **Roles** dropdown to show all project roles that have been created in your instance. Project roles are created at a global level. To add a new project role, you must be a Jira administrator. Then, go to **Settings** | **System** | **Project roles**.

6. The search box allows you to search for groups and users if you have a long list of people who appear on your screen. Or you can click on the **Roles** dropdown and select a single role or multiple roles to see the groups/users who have that role.

To add persons to your project, simply click on the **Add people** button in the top right. For our example, we will add the `Staff Meeting Access` group that we created earlier to the **Team** role:

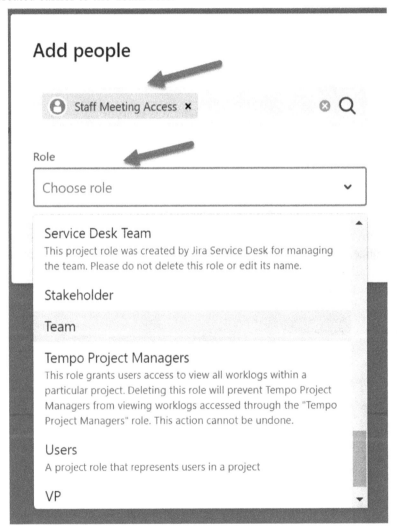

Figure 8.11 – Adding people

7. In the **Add people** dialogue box, simply add a group or username in the top box
    and then select the role for the user.

Important Note

You can only select a single role when adding a new person or group.

---

8. Once a new person or group has been added with a role, you can then update
    that person/group to associate additional roles, including adding multiple roles
    at one time:

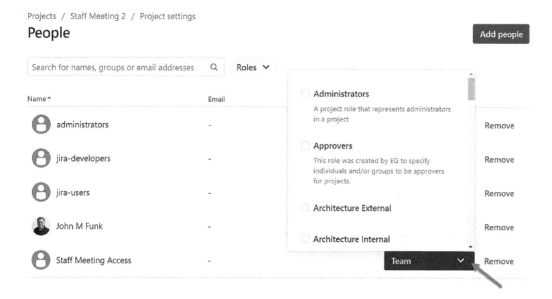

Figure 8.12 – Adding roles to a user

Adding users or groups to project roles is the preferred method to control access to your
project. In this manner, project administrators have direct control of granting access to
users. Conversely, modifying the permission scheme requires the higher role level of the
Jira administrator to make any changes.

Speaking of which, let's turn our attention to *configuring the permissions scheme.*

Configuring the permission scheme

You can access the permission scheme in two different ways. Both begin by entering **Project settings**, as shown in *Figure 8.13*.

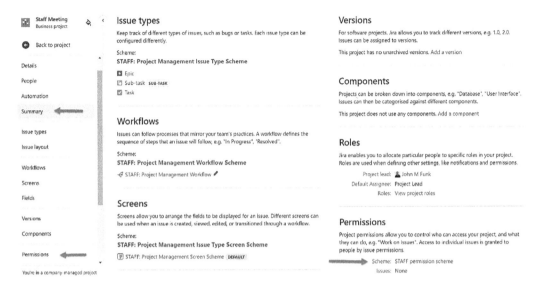

Figure 8.13 – Configuring the permission scheme

Once in the project settings, you can click on the **Summary** option in the left-hand menu and then select the permission scheme name under the **Permissions** section of **Summary**.

Alternatively, you can select the **Permissions** option from the left-hand menu to directly enter the scheme. See *Figure 8.13* for clarity on selecting either of these options.

> **Important Note**
>
> Remember that if you are on the free plan, you are not able to modify the permission scheme. All users under the free plan are automatically project administrators on all projects. Only paid plans allow the permission scheme to be modified. The following sections assume a paid plan.

Once you enter the permission scheme, you can peruse all permissions for the project and which users, groups, or project roles have been granted those permissions. You have two options at this time – the first is to **edit the permissions** in the scheme, meaning modifying which users, groups, or project roles are linked to the permission. Secondly, you can **link the project** to a different permission scheme. The latter means that the new permission scheme would be a shared scheme:

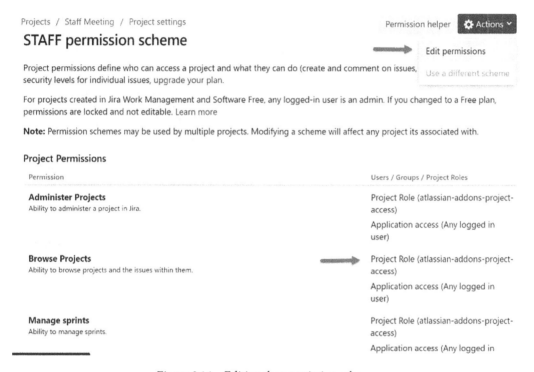

Figure 8.14 – Editing the permission scheme

Note that if you have any marketplace apps in your instance, there will be a project role added to all permission schemes for the project role of **Atlassian-addons-project-access**. This is necessary for the app to function properly and make the needed issue changes on your project:

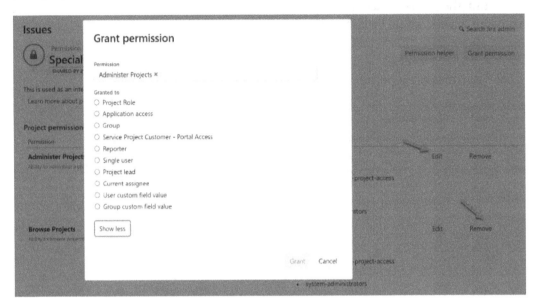

Figure 8.15 – Granting permissions

Clicking on the **Edit permissions** option will take you to the dialogue box in *Figure 8.15*. To remove any current permissions, simply click the **Remove** link and select the permission to remove. To add a new permission, click the **Edit** option, which will display the **Grant permission** popup screen.

There are several options that can be granted, as also shown in *Figure 8.15*. Once you have made the selection, click the **Grant** button at the bottom of the screen.

Permission helper

Once your permissions are all in place as desired, you might still have problems that arise with individual users not having permissions to issues on your project.

> **Important Note**
> It would not be over-exaggerating that Atlassian has provided a very supportive function for tracking down the problem.

To use the function, click on the **Permission helper** option, as shown previously in *Figure 8.14*. When the **Permission helper** screen is displayed, simply populate the **User**, **Issue**, and **Permission** fields, and click the **Submit** button at the bottom of the screen:

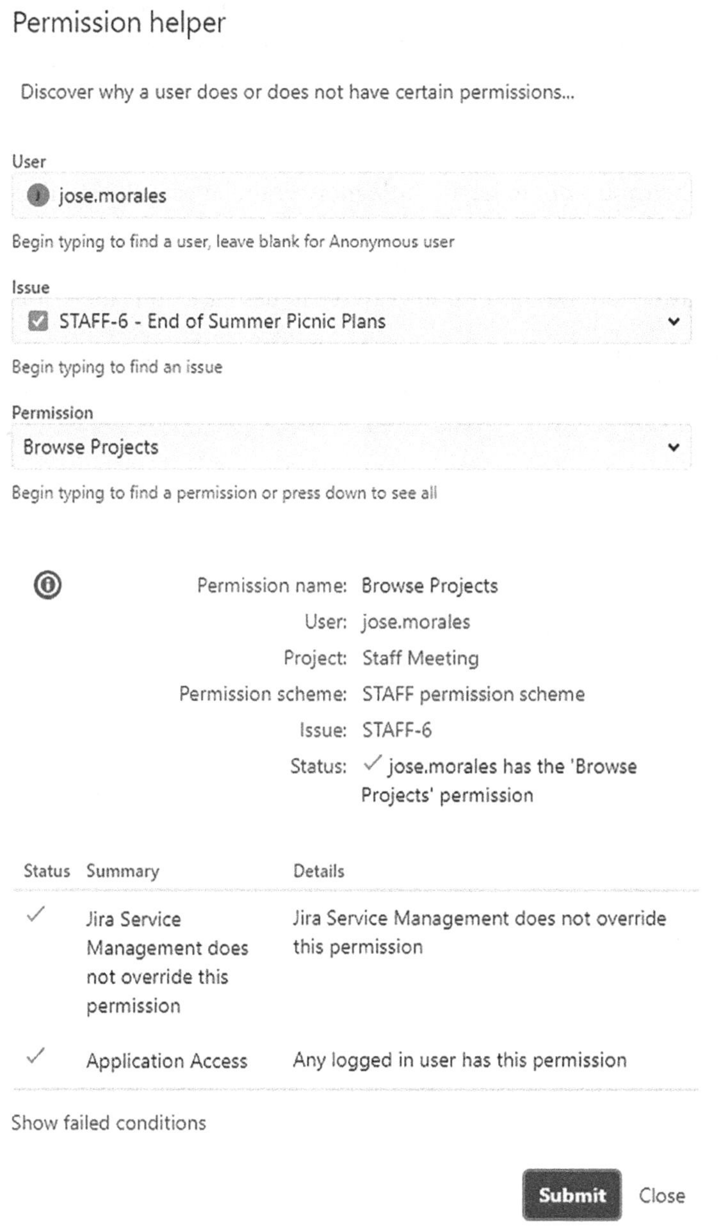

Permission helper

Discover why a user does or does not have certain permissions...

User

> jose.morales

Begin typing to find a user, leave blank for Anonymous user

Issue

> ✓ STAFF-6 - End of Summer Picnic Plans   ⌄

Begin typing to find an issue

Permission

> Browse Projects   ⌄

Begin typing to find a permission or press down to see all

Permission name:	Browse Projects
User:	jose.morales
Project:	Staff Meeting
Permission scheme:	STAFF permission scheme
Issue:	STAFF-6
Status:	✓ jose.morales has the 'Browse Projects' permission

Status	Summary	Details
✓	Jira Service Management does not override this permission	Jira Service Management does not override this permission
✓	Application Access	Any logged in user has this permission

Show failed conditions

Submit   Close

Figure 8.16 – Permission helper

The bottom of the screen will then display a verification that the user already has access or will show the recommendations on how to remedy the problem. **Permission helper** is available for both free and paid plans.

In our final section, we will explore how to apply security down to the issue level that will allow different users to have access to different issues on the same project.

Applying issue-level security

There are times when you want to have a little more granular security applied to your project. Some examples of this include the desire that reporters of issues can only see the issues that they have created and no other issues, that assignees of an issue can only see their issues, or only certain groups of users can see issues based on labels or components.

This can all be implemented using **issue security**. To access this function, enter **Project settings** and then select **Issue Security** on the left-hand menu, as shown in the following screenshot:

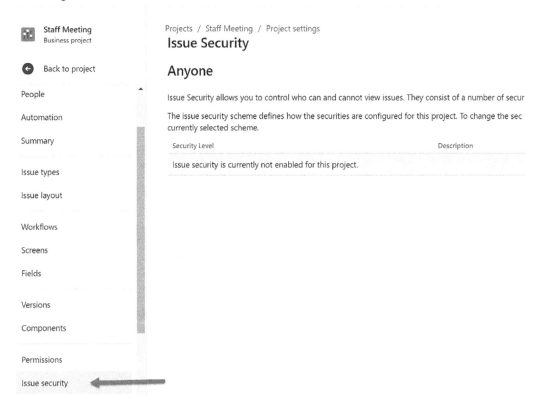

Figure 8.17 – Issue Security

For free plan users, this is how the screen would look:

Projects / Staff Meeting / Project settings

Issue Security

Anyone

🔧 Actions ˅

Issue Security allows you to control who can and cannot view issues. They consist of a number of security users/groups assigned to them.

Select a scheme

The issue security scheme defines how the securities are configured for this project. To chan different issue security scheme, or modify the currently selected scheme.

Issue-level security isn't editable on the Free plan. Upgrade for advanced access control.

Security Level	Description
Issue security is currently not enabled for this project.	

Try it now • Learn more

Figure 8.18 – Issue Security for free plan users

> **Note for Figure 8.16**
> Free plans do not have the ability to alter permissions within your instance, including issue security.

For the paid version, when you desire to add an issue security scheme to your project, you must first create the scheme through the global permissions path, meaning you must be a Jira administrator to create the scheme. Go to **Settings | Issues | Issue security schemes**. Once there, you will see a list of existing security schemes (if any exist), and at the bottom of the list will be an **Add issue security scheme** button:

Figure 8.19 – Add issue security scheme

At this point, you can insert the name of your new scheme and add a description if you like. When complete, click the **Add** button to create the scheme, as shown in *Figure 8.20*:

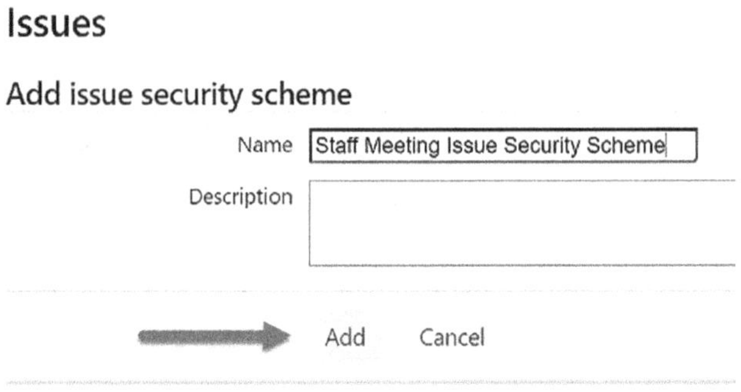

Figure 8.20 – Issue security scheme name

After the new issue security scheme has been created, you will need to return to **Project settings** for the project and select **Issue security** on the left-hand menu, as shown previously in *Figure 8.21*. Once on the **Issue security** screen, click the **Actions** menu and choose the **Select a scheme** option to link your new scheme to the project:

Figure 8.21 – Linking a security scheme to the project

After linking the scheme to the project, the options under the **Actions** menu look very similar to the options that were available for the permission scheme. You can connect this project to a different-issue security scheme, which might be already connected to another project. Thus, you would be sharing the scheme.

Sharing a scheme helps with the maintenance of your system in that you can make the change in one place instead of two (or three or four, or more!). In our company, we have dozens of product team projects linked to the same shared scheme. If you decide to share a scheme across projects, this would be the place to make that change. Your other option is to edit the current issue security scheme, as shown in *Figure 8.22*:

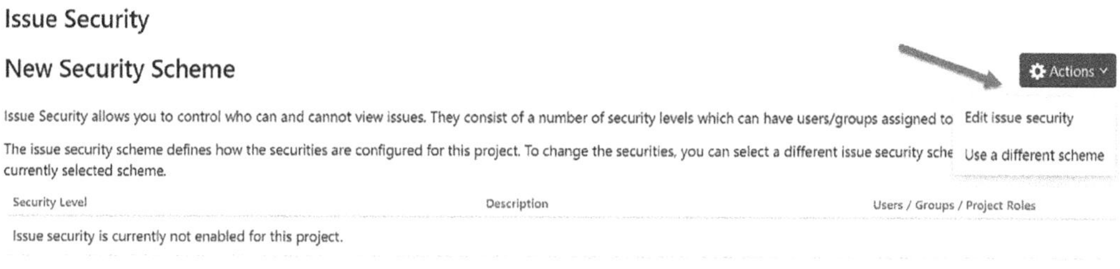

Issue Security

New Security Scheme   ⚙ Actions ⌄

Issue Security allows you to control who can and cannot view issues. They consist of a number of security levels which can have users/groups assigned to Edit issue security

The issue security scheme defines how the securities are configured for this project. To change the securities, you can select a different issue security sche Use a different scheme
currently selected scheme.

Security Level   Description   Users / Groups / Project Roles

Issue security is currently not enabled for this project.

Figure 8.22 – Editing issue security

After clicking on the **Edit issue security** option, you will need to create a new security level for the new scheme. You can have multiple security levels within each scheme, which gives you the ability to have different security policies for different issues on your project.

Give your security level a name and add a description if you like. When ready, click the **Add Security Level** button to create the security level:

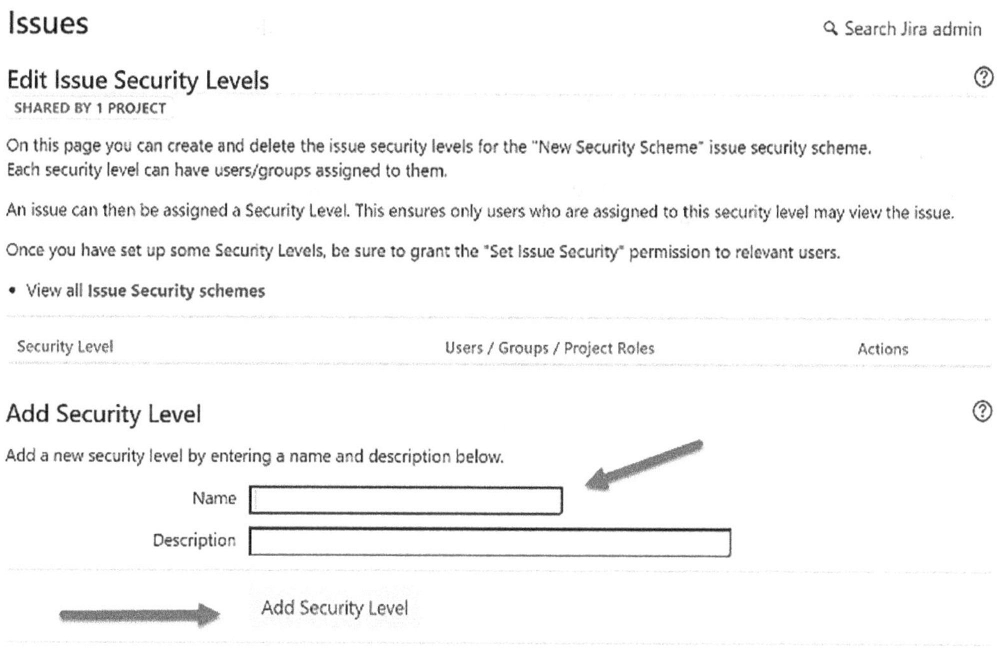

Issues   🔍 Search Jira admin

Edit Issue Security Levels   ⑦
SHARED BY 1 PROJECT

On this page you can create and delete the issue security levels for the "New Security Scheme" issue security scheme.
Each security level can have users/groups assigned to them.

An issue can then be assigned a Security Level. This ensures only users who are assigned to this security level may view the issue.

Once you have set up some Security Levels, be sure to grant the "Set Issue Security" permission to relevant users.

• View all **Issue Security schemes**

Security Level   Users / Groups / Project Roles   Actions

Add Security Level   ⑦

Add a new security level by entering a name and description below.

Name   [   ]

Description [   ]

Add Security Level

Figure 8.23 – Adding a security level

Once the new level has been created, you will need to click the **Add** button to identify who has access to this security level:

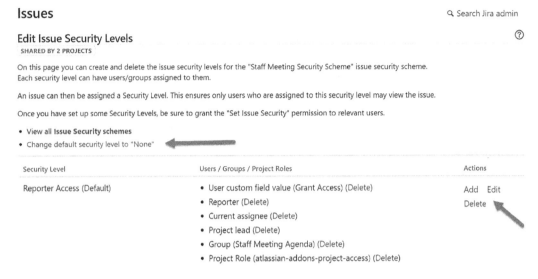

Issues   Q Search Jira admin

Edit Issue Security Levels
SHARED BY 2 PROJECTS

On this page you can create and delete the issue security levels for the "Staff Meeting Security Scheme" issue security scheme. Each security level can have users/groups assigned to them.

An issue can then be assigned a Security Level. This ensures only users who are assigned to this security level may view the issue.

Once you have set up some Security Levels, be sure to grant the "Set Issue Security" permission to relevant users.

- View all **Issue Security** schemes
- Change default security level to "None"

Security Level	Users / Groups / Project Roles	Actions
Reporter Access (Default)	• User custom field value (Grant Access) (Delete) • Reporter (Delete) • Current assignee (Delete) • Project lead (Delete) • Group (Staff Meeting Agenda) (Delete) • Project Role (atlassian-addons-project-access) (Delete)	Add Edit Delete

Figure 8.24 – Issue security options

The result will be a dialogue box that allows you to add persons to the security level by including a single user, groups, values in custom fields, project roles, and so on. For example, clicking on **Group** and adding the value of administrators gives all persons with Jira administrator permissions access to the issues attached to that level.

Other examples would be selecting **Reporter** or **Assignee**, which would allow whichever user is currently in those fields to see and access the issue. In other words, if the user is not the reporter or the assignee, they will not be able to even see the issue:

Issues

Add User/Group/Project Role to Issue Security Level

Issue Security Scheme: **Staff Meeting Security Scheme**
Issue Security Level: **Reporter Access**

Please select a user or group to add to this security level.
This will enable the specific users/groups to view issues for projects that:

- are associated with this Issue Security Scheme and
- have their security level set to **Reporter Access**

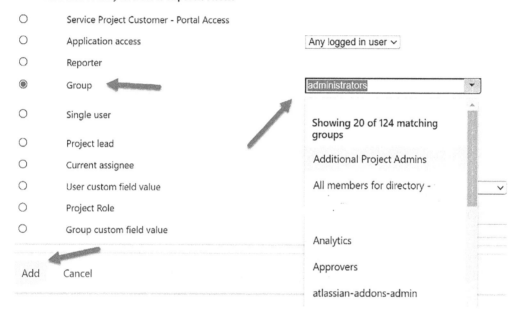

Figure 8.25 – Editing the issue security

It is suggested that you add at least one security level as the default for the scheme if using issue security. This will ensure that all newly created issues will be attached to a security level. See *Figure 8.24* for the location of the link to the default value.

Now that we can secure our project and provide access to select persons, let's look at some other functions that can be done as a project administrator.

JWM project administrator capabilities

Possessing project administration permissions sounds impressive, but there are not actually many functions that the administrator can perform. In fact, the list is rather small. Or course, most permission schemes will grant special permissions to project administrators that other users or project roles will not have.

The following highlights the most used or known aspects of the capabilities of a project administrator but is not intended to be an exhaustive list. You can find more information by searching in Atlassian's own documentation, but this will help get you started:

- **Project roles**: As discussed earlier in this chapter in the *Project roles and permissions* section, project administrators can add users to a project and place them in different roles.

- **Components**: Components are unique to each project and help to categorize work being done on the project. Project administrators can create and delete components on their projects.

- **Versions and releases**: As with components, versions and releases are unique to a project and can be added and deleted by project administrators.

- **Issue layout and screens**: If the screen is exclusively used on a single project, the project administrator will be able to make a few changes. However, the project administrator will have the ability to make changes directly in the issue layout, as discussed previously in *Chapter 7, Managing Fields, Screens, and Issue Layouts*.

- **Workflows**: Similar to screens, project administrators can make changes to workflows if the workflow is uniquely associated with one project.

And now we wrap up this chapter with a brief look and recap of functions that are available to Jira administrators and project administrators.

Jira administrators versus project administrators

Again, this is not intended to be an exhaustive list, and you can search Atlassian's documentation for more details. However, you can relate Jira administrator functions to be more global in nature, meaning they affect the entire Jira instance/site.

Jira administrators can make changes to shared schemes (workflows, screens, and issue types), create custom fields, edit the permission scheme, change ownership of shared dashboards and filters, and other system-level functions.

For JWM, project administrators can make changes to non-shared objects and project roles on the project, but not the permission scheme used by the project. *Figure 8.26* shows a very brief table of permissions available for Jira administrators and project administrators. In a nutshell, Jira administrators can make changes globally within your Jira instance and project administrators can only make changes on the projects where they have the project administrator role:

Jira administrator	Project administrator
Create projects	Add/edit project components
Create project roles	Create/edit project releases/versions
Add users and groups to the Jira instance	Add existing users to a project and place them in project roles
Create and modify shared schemes such as permissions, workflows, and screens	Modify simple workflows only used by their project
Create custom fields	Create/modify project automations

Figure 8.26 – Jira administrator versus project administrator permissions

All of these come with a caveat for free subscriptions in that all users in the instance are project administrators.

New terms learned in this chapter

Let's conclude the chapter by going through the list of new terms learned in this chapter:

- **Jira administrator**: The Jira administrator can make all changes at the system and project level within your Jira instance for the products the user has been granted access to.

- **Organization administrator**: The organization administrator can add other organization administrators, create system-level API keys, verify domains for your site, implement Atlassian Access, and control the directory of managed users for your domain.

- **Site administrator**: The site administrator can activate or deactivate users' access to products in your instance by inviting them to the instance. He/she can also create groups and assign users to those groups.

- **Free plan**: A no-cost JWM plan that is limited to 10 active users and does not have configurable permissions.

- **Paid plan**: There are various plans available for JWM for different levels of users. All come with the most flexible options for the administrator of your JWM product.

- **Issue security**: Security that can be applied at the issue level to completely grant access to or hide issues from users.

- **Project roles**: Project administrators can add users to a project and place them in different roles.

- **Components**: Components are unique to each project and help to categorize work being done on the project.

- **Versions and releases**: Versions and releases are unique to a project and can be added and deleted by project administrators. They group issues by release and can be used to remove issues from boards.

Summary

In this chapter, we have learned how site administrators can invite new users to your Jira organization and how project administrators can add users to a project and associate them with roles to grant them permissions to the project. We also learned about the permission scheme and how it relates to project roles, groups, and users.

Then, we delved into additional security capabilities using issue-level security as a layer on top of the permission scheme. And, finally, we learned some of the different functions that Jira administrators and project administrators can perform and what is unique to each role.

In the next chapter, we will learn how to migrate existing Jira projects to JWM projects, use shared schemes, and work with external functions.

9
Duplicating Projects and Starting Outside the Box

So far, we have explored and learned how to get up and running with **Jira Work Management** (**JWM**) quickly by making use of the standard or out-of-the-box functions of JWM. This typically means creating projects and issues directly in the product by simply clicking on a few buttons and adding some text.

This chapter will venture off the beaten path and look at ways to create issues from outside of the tool. This provides us with flexibility as to how our customers and internal teammates can get work requests to us and removes some of the friction when starting new work.

If you have already been using the Jira Software and/or **Jira Service Management** (**JSM**) projects but want to take advantage of the cool new features of JWM with your existing work, we will learn how to migrate existing projects to JWM. Finally, we will have one more look at a Marketplace app to help with creating issues based on existing issues.

In this chapter, we are going to cover the following main topics:

- Creating a project based on an existing project
- Using shared schemes
- Creating issues externally
- Migrating existing Jira projects to JWM
- Working with Marketplace apps – Deep Clone for Jira

By completing this chapter, you will have learned how to create a new project based on an existing project and how to mimic that using shared schemes. You will have also learned some alternative methods to creating issues from outside of the system and how to migrate projects within Jira to JWM.

Let's get started!

Technical requirements

As JWM is only available in the Jira Cloud environment, the requirement for this chapter is simple: *you must have access to a Jira Cloud environment.*

Atlassian provides a free JWM account for up to 10 users. You can create an account by going to `https://www.atlassian.com/try/cloud/signup?bundle=jira-core&edition=free` and following the instructions provided.

Creating a project based on an existing project

Although we have seen that the availability of project templates is numerous for quickly creating projects in JWM, we will often tweak those initial settings once the project has been created. This might entail modifying the workflow or adjusting/adding fields to the screen.

At this stage, it may be helpful if subsequent similar projects that we create make use of the changes we have made. In effect, we have created a new *template* for our project. So, the question is, how can we create new projects using the changed objects that are attached to existing projects?

The answer is to create a new project based on the existing project. Let's learn how to do this:

1. First, we will begin as we normally would; that is, by clicking on the **Projects** option from the top navigation bar and selecting **Create project**:

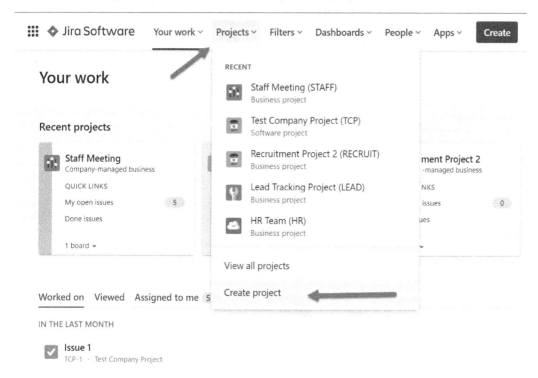

Figure 9.1 – Creating a project

2. This leads us to the group of JWM templates we saw in *Chapter 2, Working with Project Templates*. To investigate an alternative route to these templates, let's click on **Jira Work Management**, which can be found at the bottom left of the screen.

3. Once again, a list of all the JWM project templates will be displayed, as shown in the following screenshot. In our scenario, let's say we want to create a new project for the technology division's monthly meetings. We have decided that it should follow the same pattern we have already set up for our Staff Meeting project. From here, we must select **Project management**:

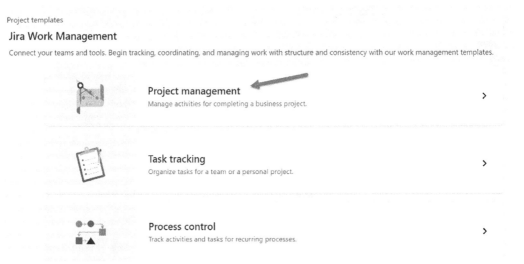

Figure 9.2 – JWM project templates

4. As soon as we arrive on the next screen, we can simply click on the **Use template** button at the top or bottom of the screen:

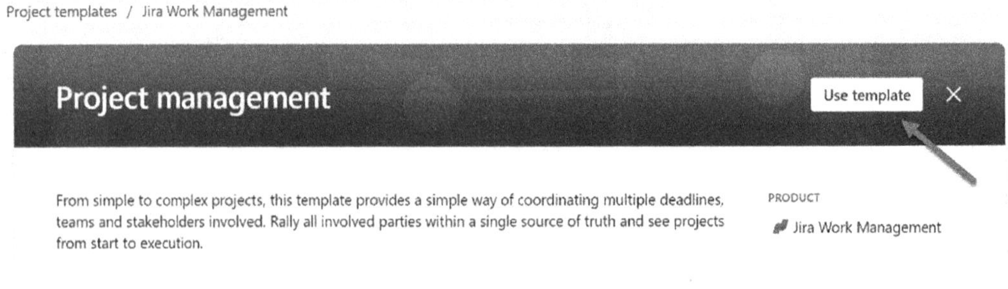

Figure 9.3 – Use template

5. Finally, the **Add project details** screen will be displayed. Note that, once again, you will encounter a difference if you are using the free subscription. Creating a project based on an existing project is not available for those plans:

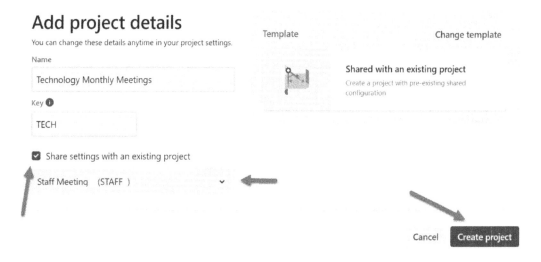

Add project details

You can change these details anytime in your project settings.

Name

Try a team name, project goal, milestone...

Key

Share settings with an existing project

Share project settings aren't available on
Free plan. Upgrade to save time on project
setup.

Template   Change template

Project management

Manage activities for completing a business
project.

Cancel   Create project

Figure 9.4 – Add project details

6.   Let's continue by looking at the process for those with a paid subscription. Enter
     a **Name** for the new project, as well as the project's **Key**, as you normally would.
     However, there's a twist to this: check the box for **Share settings with an existing
     project**, as shown in the preceding screenshot.

7.   Checking this box will give you access to a dropdown field. Click on that field
     and scroll down to select the project that you would like to base your new project
     on. For our example, we will select the **Staff Meeting** project. After that, click the
     Create project button to finish creating the project:

Add project details

You can change these details anytime in your project settings.

Name

Technology Monthly Meetings

Key

TECH

☑ Share settings with an existing project

Staff Meeting   (STAFF)

Template   Change template

Shared with an existing project

Create a project with pre-existing shared
configuration

Cancel   Create project

Figure 9.5 – Create project

8. Once the project has been created, you will be dropped onto the project's new board, as we saw in *Chapter 3, Creating Your First Project*. Notice the name of the new project in the top breadcrumbs section. Also, notice that this looks just like the board that was created for our original **Staff Meeting** project:

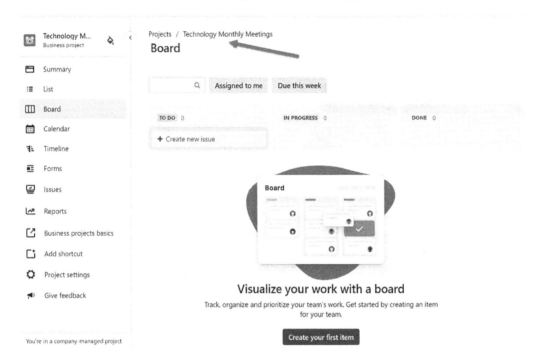

Figure 9.6 – Your new project

If we proceed to the **Summary** section of **Project settings** for the **Technology Monthly Meetings** project, we will see that this new project uses the same schemes as the **Staff Meeting** project. In effect, these schemes have now become **shared schemes** because more than one project uses each of those schemes. The following screenshot shows the new project using the Staff Meeting project-related schemes:

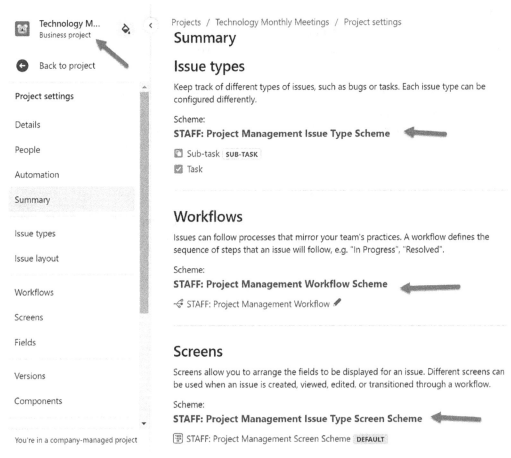

Figure 9.7 – Shared schemes

Since creating new projects in this manner is not available for those on a free plan, let's look at an alternative to achieve similar results. What we are about to see with shared schemes will work with any Jira Work Management, JSM, or Jira Software company-managed type of project.

Using shared schemes

Shared schemes are a great way to bring consistency to projects in your organization and reduce the maintenance needs for your Jira administrators. Having multiple projects use a single shared scheme allows you to change the scheme once and have it automatically update all the connected projects.

In my organization, we try to use shared schemes as often as possible. This might mean being a little creative with workflows to include statuses and transitions that use conditions based on the project's name or role. But once you have done that, it becomes easier the next time.

Updating the schemes on a free plan project can achieve the same result as a **shared project template**; it will just take a few extra steps. Note that we can do this with most shared schemes for the free plan, except for the permission scheme. As we saw in the previous chapter, *Chapter 8, Configuring Permissions and Simple Administration*, you cannot modify the permission scheme for free subscriptions.

So, how does this work? Let's take a look:

1. Once again, we begin by navigating to the **Project settings** area and then the **Summary** section. As shown in the following screenshot, you can click on any of the schemes to make a change:

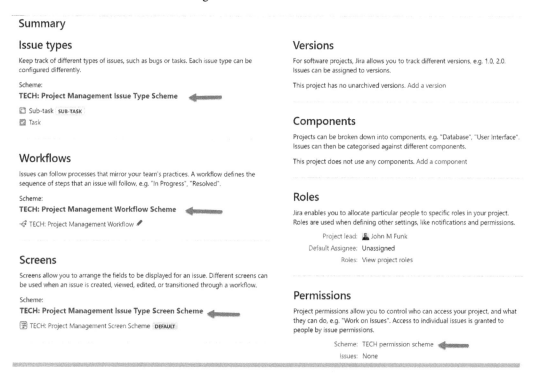

Summary

Issue types

Keep track of different types of issues, such as bugs or tasks. Each issue type can be configured differently.

Scheme:
TECH: Project Management Issue Type Scheme

☑ Sub-task SUB-TASK
☑ Task

Workflows

Issues can follow processes that mirror your team's practices. A workflow defines the sequence of steps that an issue will follow, e.g. "In Progress", "Resolved".

Scheme:
TECH: Project Management Workflow Scheme

⚡ TECH: Project Management Workflow ✏

Screens

Screens allow you to arrange the fields to be displayed for an issue. Different screens can be used when an issue is created, viewed, edited, or transitioned through a workflow.

Scheme:
TECH: Project Management Issue Type Screen Scheme

▣ TECH: Project Management Screen Scheme DEFAULT

Versions

For software projects, Jira allows you to track different versions, e.g. 1.0, 2.0. Issues can be assigned to versions.

This project has no unarchived versions. Add a version

Components

Projects can be broken down into components, e.g. "Database", "User Interface". Issues can then be categorised against different components.

This project does not use any components. Add a component

Roles

Jira enables you to allocate particular people to specific roles in your project. Roles are used when defining other settings, like notifications and permissions.

Project lead: 👤 John M Funk
Default Assignee: Unassigned
Roles: View project roles

Permissions

Project permissions allow you to control who can access your project, and what they can do, e.g. "Work on Issues". Access to individual issues is granted to people by issue permissions.

Scheme: TECH permission scheme
Issues: None

Figure 9.8 – Changing shared schemes

2. Depending on which scheme you are looking to change, the process might be slightly different. For **TECH: Project Management Issue Type Scheme**, you will enter the scheme, then click the **Actions** button, and finally select **Use a different scheme**, as shown in the following screenshot. Then, you must select the scheme you want to use from the resulting list:

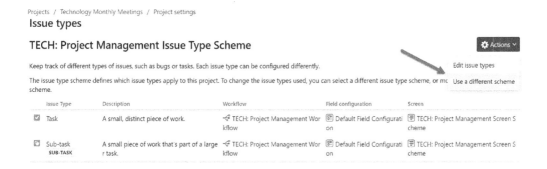

Figure 9.9 – Issue Type Scheme

3. For **TECH: Project Management Workflow Scheme**, you must click on the **Switch Scheme** button and select the new scheme instead:

Figure 9.10 – Workflow Scheme

4.   Again, for our example, we will use the Staff Meeting-related scheme:

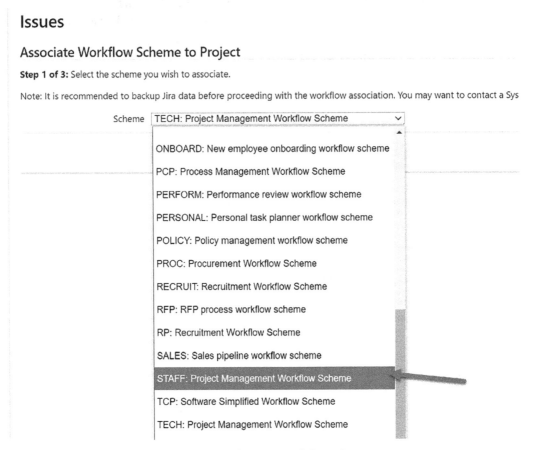

Figure 9.11 – Selecting a workflow scheme

5.   For the new workflow scheme selection, you will be required to associate all the existing issues in your project with the new workflow(s).

Now that we know how to change our schemes so that we can share them, let's look at alternative ways we can create issues.

Creating issues externally

As we have mentioned previously, issues represent the work we do on our projects. They may manifest themselves as cards on a board or simply as a row in a list for the project. All of that tells us that issues are unique objects and belong to the project, not the list or the board. In other words, you do not create an issue on a board or a list – you create an issue against a project.

We are not going to go into the details of each of the following methods, but this list is intended to give you a high-level familiarity with the possibilities. Where appropriate, we have added links to further details about each method. But suffice it to say that each of these processes will allow you to create issues on your project from outside of your JWM product:

- **Email**: This function will allow your users to create cards by simply sending an email to a prearranged email address in your organization. The sender of the email will be captured as the *Reporter*, the subject of the email will be the *Summary*, and the body of the email will be placed in the *Description* field of the issue. See `https://support.atlassian.com/jira-cloud-administration/docs/create-issues-and-comments-from-email/` for more details. There are also free and paid apps in the Atlassian Marketplace to perform this process.

- **Slack**: Slack is a favorite tool for many companies due to how easily internal chats can take place. Atlassian and Slack have teamed up to produce some excellent integration between the products, including the ability to create Jira issues from comments/discussions inside of Slack. This requires a free app to be installed. See `https://www.atlassian.com/software/jira/guides/expand-jira/jira-slack-integration` for more information.

- **Microsoft Teams**: Very similar to the Slack integration, Microsoft and Atlassian have connected to bring you a free app to connect the two tools. Besides issue creation, you can display lists of Jira issues and/or boards directly in a Teams tab. See `https://marketplace.atlassian.com/apps/1217836/microsoft-teams-for-jira?tab=overview&hosting=cloud` for more information.

- **REST API call**: Though more technical, this option will provide the most flexibility as to the amount of information that can be created in a new issue. It is strongly suggested that you have some type of development background to attempt this. See `https://blog.developer.atlassian.com/creating-a-jira-cloud-issue-in-a-single-rest-call/` for more information.

It is awesome to see so many ways to create issues for your JWM project. But what if you already have other projects in Jira and want to use JWM's features? Let's see how we can migrate those.

Migrating existing Jira projects to Jira Work Management

As we outlined in our very first chapter, *Chapter 1, Why Choose Jira Work Management?*, part of the target audience for this book is both those completely new to Jira and those who have used Jira before but are not familiar with the new JWM product.

As such, some of you may already have existing projects that use other Jira project types. And now, having seen the new features and capabilities of JWM, perhaps you would like to move some of your projects over to the new product. Remember that you cannot simply convert project types – you must create a new project and migrate issues from the old project to the new project.

If you have already done some project migrations before, this will not be anything new for you. But for those who have not, let's take a look. We will follow a basic flow that we will outline first and then add screenshots as we progress to reinforce the process:

1. **Create a new JWM project**: This can be any JWM project type you desire. Just use a template and off you go!

2. **Map any existing custom fields in your project to the new project**: In the *Custom fields* section of *Chapter 7, Managing Fields, Screens, and Issue Layouts*, we discussed how to modify the context of the custom field to add projects. You should do this for any custom fields on your existing non-JWM project to add the new JWM project you just created.

3. **Add any custom fields to your JWM project screen**: At this point, you must add these custom fields to the screen that will be used by your new JWM project.

4. **Execute a basic or advanced filter search**: Execute a simple search, as shown in *Figure 9.13*.

5. **Perform a bulk change to move the existing issues to the new project**: Finally, bulk move the existing issues to the new project.

For our example, we will move issues from the **Staff Meeting** project to the **Technology Monthly Meetings** project. First, click on the **Search** box in the top navigation bar:

Figure 9.12 – The search box

At this point, you can do a basic search by changing the project on the far left to your existing project (Staff Meeting, for our example). Alternatively, you can click the **Switch to JQL** button and perform an advanced search. Your code will resemble `Project = STAFF`. Then, click **Search**:

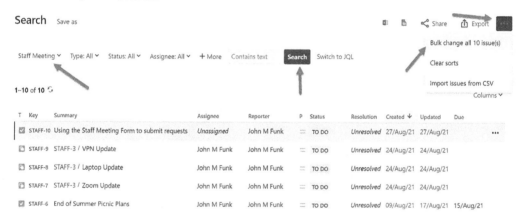

Figure 9.13 –Search and the Bulk change option

Once you have a list of all the issues in the project, click the ellipsis menu (…) at the top right and select the **Bulk change** option. Select all of the issues, and then select **Move**:

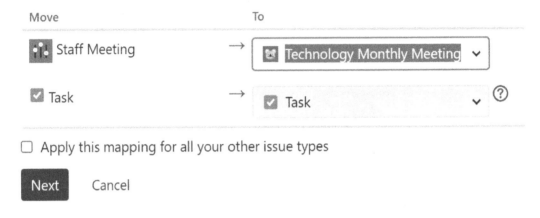

Figure 9.14 – Performing a bulk move

Change the **To** project to your new JWM project, click **Next**, and then follow the prompts. When the migration is complete, all of your old project's issues will have been moved to your JWM project!

Finally, we will learn how another Atlassian Marketplace app can help you be more productive.

Working with Marketplace apps – Deep Clone for Jira

As we saw in *Chapter 4, Modifying the Board, Workflow, and Associated Schemes*, Atlassian Marketplace apps can bring some very helpful functionality to our JWM projects by extending the capabilities of the built-in tools.

So, we will continue that spirit here with the Marketplace app called **Deep Clone for Jira**. Earlier, in the *Creating issues externally* section, we learned how to create issues outside of the normal **Create** button process. With Deep Clone, we can create issues by cloning existing issues.

Jira has a built-in clone process, but it does not provide much flexibility. Namely, you can only clone an issue into the same project, and you cannot adjust any fields in the new issue during the cloning process.

What sets Deep Clone apart is its ability to modify all the fields that are available in the create screen for the new issue, regardless of the project you are cloning into. So, you can clone an issue from Project A to Project B and modify the values of the fields in Project A so that they're different values in the new issue in Project B. You can also bulk clone issues, clone comments, subtasks, and even epics and their related children. Here's how to find more information on the app.

Since Deep Clone can also clone multiple objects at the same time, it can be used to create several new issues of varying types (epics, stories, tasks, subtasks, and more) in a single process. This is perhaps the closest you can come to creating what could be considered a custom template (in addition to the standard out-of-the-box templates):

Figure 9.15 – Deep Clone for Jira

You can find out more about Deep Clone for Jira at https://bit.ly/3tPqFTD.

Summary

In this chapter, we learned how to create a new project by utilizing the components of an existing project and how to achieve similar results using shared schemes. We also saw some alternative methods to creating issues from outside of Jira using various third-party applications and tools.

Then, we learned how to migrate existing Jira projects into JWM projects to begin using JWM's features. Finally, we learned about the Deep Clone for Jira Marketplace app and how it can extend functionality by cloning issues into other projects and modifying fields in the process.

With these new skills, you will be able to add flexibility to how you approach project and issue creation. This might eliminate the need for you to have to jump back and forth between applications to create issues.

In the next chapter, we will learn how to leverage the Automation for Jira tool to automate routine tasks and add power to our projects and issues.

10
Using Project Automation

To draw on a food analogy, so far you have had your appetizer, salad, and main course over the first nine chapters of this book. And now, I consider **project automation** to be our dessert!

Automation can bring incredible power to your **Jira Work Management (JWM)** project and the work associated with it.

Maybe you want to automate routine and/or repetitive tasks. Maybe you want to auto-assign work to dedicated users, or even create a round-robin schedule for your team assignments. Maybe you want the system to keep subtasks synchronized with their parent. Or maybe you even want to use a formula to calculate a new value based on the sum of multiple fields.

Regardless of what excites you most about automation, you can eat your fill of a variety of automated goodness. All with the simplicity of a tool that is mostly point-and-click, with no coding needed!

In this chapter, you will learn about the concept of automation, including what it is and how it can be used. You will also learn how to create simple automation rules to become immediately productive. As well as creating these rules, you will also learn how to access existing automation templates that will give you an even more powerful start.

Finally, you will learn about some common automation use cases, such as synchronizing parent and children *issues*, auto-assigning work, scheduling rules, and sending emails.

In this chapter, we are going to cover the following main topics:

- What is automation?
- Creating automation rules
- Using automation templates
- Common automation use cases

Technical requirements

As JWM is only available in the **Jira Cloud** environment, the technical requirements for this chapter are simple:

- Access to the Jira Cloud environment

If you already have access to Jira Cloud, that's great – you are ready to go! If not, **Atlassian** provides a free JWM account for up to 10 users. You can create your account by following the instructions at `https://www.atlassian.com/try/cloud/signup?bundle=jira-core&edition=free`.

Now, let's get started.

What is automation?

Automation is a tool provided with all Jira Cloud instances as part of any type of subscription you have. It can extend your JWM work by simplifying the manual processes that you need to perform.

Automation works by creating point and click rules which contain triggers, conditions and actions. These rules can be very powerful in the amount of time it saves you by reducing extra manual edits and calculations.

However, we also need to mention a few limitations related to the rules. There are unlimited rule executions for single project rules – meaning the rule runs against a single project. However, there are limits or levels of executions for global or multi-project rules available in relation to your subscription type, which we will discuss later in the chapter.

Automation allows project administrators and Jira administrators to save time by setting up rules that fire based on various system events. Some examples of *system events* include the following:

- Issues transitioning from one status to another

- The updating of a field in an issue

- The creation of a new issue

- A scheduled trigger that runs at a pre-determined time or is manually executed by a user

Rules can have conditions applied that narrow their focus. These conditions can include branching for sub-groups of issues or specifying the actions that a rule can execute provides extra flexibility for conditions.

An entire book could be written about project automation in Jira, but for this chapter, we will only touch on some of the main points of the tool to get you started.

Automation rules have a standard set of components or parts which make up the steps of the rule. Next, we briefly describe each part. Later, in the *Creating automation rules* section, we will see how to create a rule using each component:

- **Triggers**: *Triggers* are the first step in your rule. They act as event listeners for the rule and will fire based on a variety of events, such as an issue being created or transitioned, the value of a field changing, or many others.

- **Conditions**: You can add an optional *condition* so that once the initial trigger fires, you can have additional checks that determine if the rule should continue to run. If the condition fails, the rule stops. These checks can be based on simple criteria such as the value of a field or date ranges. Or, you can include more complex conditions, such as advanced compares, **Jira Query Language** (**JQL**) queries, and more.

- **Actions**: Finally, *actions* result in some kind of change to your project based on the rule, such as a field value change, automatically transitioning an issue, calculating number values, assigning issues to a user, or sending an email or other notification.

Next, we will discuss how to set up automation, and you will be able to create your first rule.

Creating automation rules

There are a couple of ways to navigate to the list of rules for automation. As a Jira administrator, you have access to all rules within your Jira instance through the system settings screen. Start by clicking the gear icon in the upper right-hand corner of the top navigation bar and selecting **System**, as shown in *Figure 10.1*:

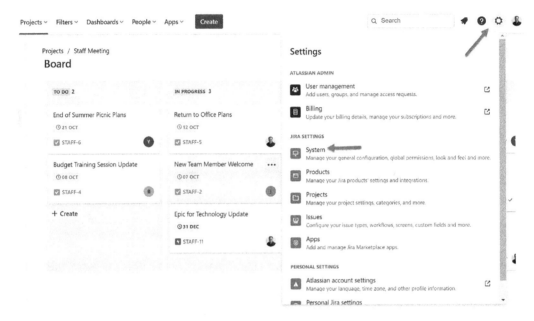

Figure 10.1 – System settings

Then scroll to the bottom of page and click **Automation rules** on the left. Clicking this will take you to the **Automation** window, where examples of rules are available organized by subject in the **Library** tab. *Figure 10.2* shows the initial **Automation** window **Library** tab, as well as the other options available for the automation tool:

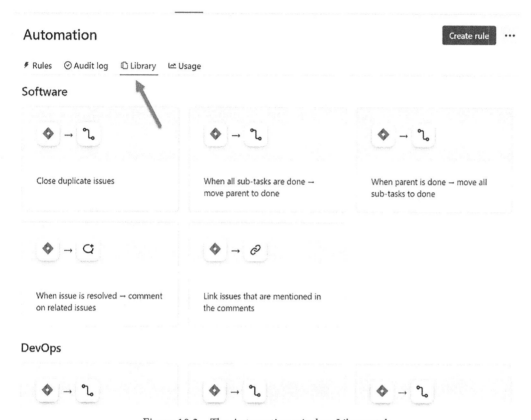

Figure 10.2 – The Automation window Library tab

The automation library can be a good starting place to see a handful of available rules and become familiar with the automation rule syntax and style. You are encouraged to look through the rules to see what's available.

Another path is limited to just rules that run against a single project. These rules are accessed through the **Project settings** window for the project.

Now, we will turn our attention to the building blocks of creating a rule. Click the **Rules** tab in the upper left, as shown in *Figure 10.3*:

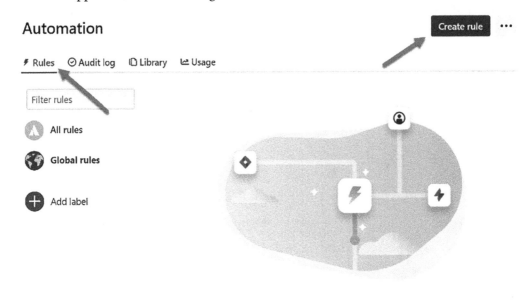

Figure 10.3 – The Automation window Rules tab

Let's walk through the process of creating a simple rule:

1. First, click the **Create rule** button in the upper right, as shown in *Figure 10.3*.

2. This brings us to the list of *triggers*, as shown in *Figure 10.4*:

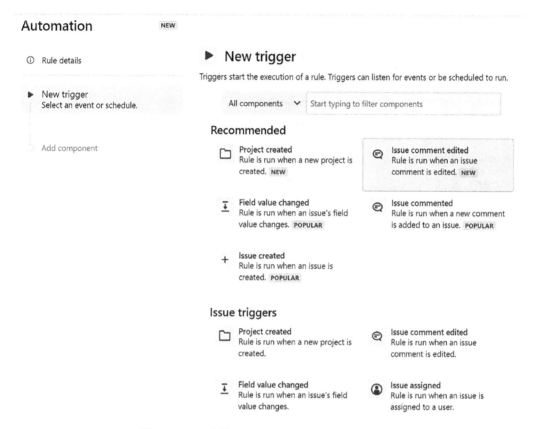

Figure 10.4 – Adding triggers to an automation rule

Here, we see some of the most popular and recommended triggers. We will select **Field value changed** for our example and base it on the **Presentation Date** field.

3. Once selected and saved, let's add a *condition*. Again, we see the recommended conditions. We will select the **Issue fields condition** option, as shown in *Figure 10.5*. For our example, we will check to see if the **Issue** status is in **Progress**. Also, notice how the rule is being generated and displayed with each part on the left-hand side:

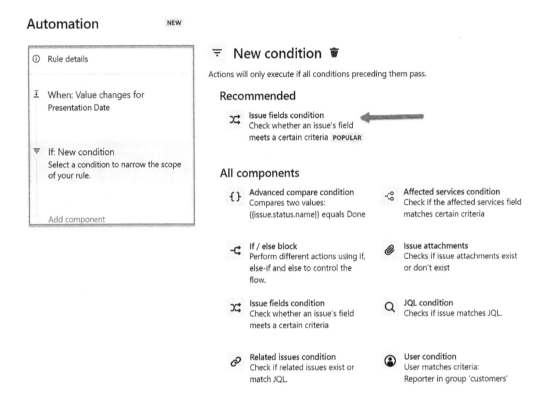

Figure 10.5 – Adding conditions to an automation rule

4. Finally, let's add a new action to send an email notifying the assignee that the issue they are working on now has a new **Presentation Date** value. We will select the **Send email** option from the available actions, as shown in *Figure 10.6*:

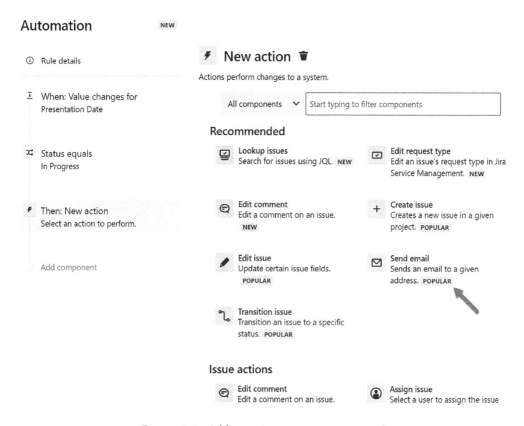

Figure 10.6 – Adding actions to an automation rule

5.   Our final step will be to save the rule and link it to a project. We will use our **Staff Meeting** project and enter the name of the rule as `Send email when Presentation Date changes`. We can see our final rule, along with the rule name and the project it links to, in *Figure 10.7*:

Figure 10.7 – Adding an automation rule name and linking a project

Next, we'll take a look at how we can make use of existing templates to get our automation going quickly.

Using automation templates

As we already saw in our discussion of *projects*, templates can provide a quick and easy way to get started with whatever type of object you are creating. This is also true of automation templates for business teams. *Figure 10.8* shows some of the default automation templates available:

Jira automation templates for business and non-tech teams

It is not just software teams that use Jira. In fact, 9 out of 10 people who use Jira automation are not developers.

Below are a few of the common use cases we have seen business teams (including Project Managers, HR, legal and marketing teams) use. All can be completely customized to your own needs.

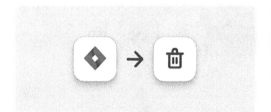

Delete attachments from old Jira issues

Using a scheduled trigger, seek out old Jira issues and delete their attachments. Perfect for those with a passion for compliance & GDPR.

Onboard / off-board employees

This is a rule commonly used by HR teams to automate the process of new hires or making sure you tick all the boxes when an employee is leaving.

Figure 10.8 – Jira automation templates

Figure 10.9 also displays additional Jira templates available for business projects. These include templates for adding security levels and a possible **Slack** integration:

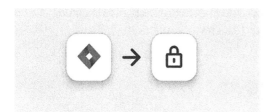

Edit security level when a confidential issue is created

Whenever a confidential issue is created, then edit the security level and comment on the issue. Legal teams, in particular, use this rule.

Go to rule →

Automate the webinar process

Whenever a 'webinar' issue is created by marketing, automatically create a design ticket with specs and a landing page ticket. Then link them altogether.

Go to rule →

Add 'approver' and send Slack when design ticket is ready

Just like developers, good designers like to stay in focus mode. This rule automates the approval process and updates the team so the designer doesn't need to.

Go to rule →

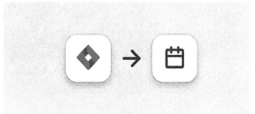

Email reporter when expense claims have no attachments

This rule is a good example of how a finance team can automate the checking of expense claims. Any issues that are in a certain status but have no attachments? Email the owner to remind them.

Go to rule →

Figure 10.9 – Jira business project templates

Automation templates will continue to be added by Atlassian as new ideas and suggestions come to light. To access the templates, go to `https://www.atlassian.com/software/jira/automation-template-library#/rule/new`.

Another handy feature is the **Jira Automation Playground**. At the bottom of the automation template website shown in *Figure 10.8* and *Figure 10.9*, there is a **Jira sandbox**. Here, you can look at many existing rules, try your hand at creating rules in a safe environment away from your production site, and generally learn the syntax for how the parts of a rule can be used. You can see the Automation Playground in *Figure 10.10*:

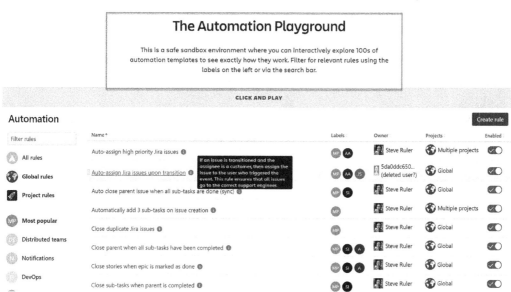

Figure 10.10 – The Jira Automation Playground

Next, we will finish the chapter by looking at some of the most common automation use cases.

Common automation use cases

Although we have already discussed automation templates and the automation library, it will help to look at some common use cases specifically. These use cases have come about based on frequent questions in the **Atlassian Community** user support environment and previous Atlassian support requests.

So, let's take a look at some of the most common ones:

- **Keeping parent issues and subtasks in sync**: As many of the JWM project templates include subtasks in the initially created issue type scheme, auto-transition of the parent tasks can be based on the movement of the subtasks. In other words, when the first subtask moves to **In Progress**, the automation rule will move the parent into the **In Progress** status. The same can happen when the final open subtask is closed, as we move the parent issue to Done, as shown in *Figure 10.11*:

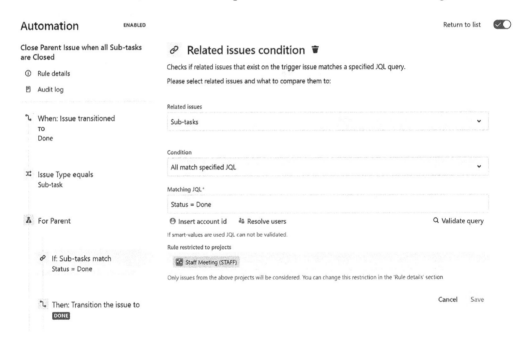

Figure 10.11 – A parent and child automation task rule

- **Assigning an issue to a user automatically when the issue is created**: There are a number of ways to automatically assign a user to an issue in JWM. However, creating an automation rule to do this allows greater flexibility – you can assign a user directly, or you can use options such as creating round-robins, balanced workloads, or even random assignments. *Figure 10.11* shows a round-robin being used:

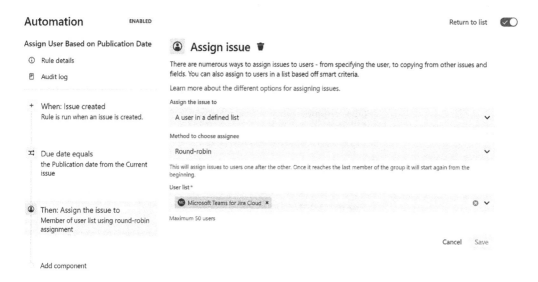

Figure 10.12 – An assign issue automation rule

- **Scheduling a process to happen at specific times**: Scheduled rules are a great way to send notifications based on date fields or other criteria from a JQL query. They can be set up to run at specific times, including on a daily, weekly, or monthly basis, or they can be more specific. This is also a great way to handle recurring tasks in your project.

Figure 10.12 shows a visual of how to set up a scheduled rule:

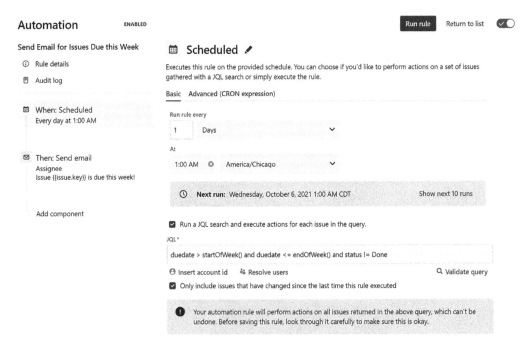

Figure 10.13 – A scheduled automation rule example

So, as you can see, automation rules can be very powerful in extending your JWM projects, but having some common automation use cases already identified and built for you can make you immediately productive.

Automation rule executions and usage limitations

Now that we see the huge benefit we can gain by using automation, let's briefly describe some potential usage limits to the number of rule executions you can perform on a monthly basis.

Global and multi-project rules represent automations that run in your entire Jira instance or against two or more projects at the same time. In this case, there is no execution usage difference for the number of projects you use in your rule, assuming there are at least two projects.

You are given an identified number of monthly rule executions for free, and after that, there are no more executions allowed for the remainder of the month for global and multi-project rules. The current usage limits can be seen in the following table:

Plan	Monthly allotment
Free	100
Standard	500
Premium	1,000 per paid premium user. For example, 300 users get 300,000 monthly executions.
Enterprise	Unlimited

Table 10.1 – Automation rule execution limits

> **Latest Plan Usage Limits**
>
> The most up-to-date usage limits can be seen at `https://support.atlassian.com/jira-cloud-administration/docs/explore-jira-cloud-plans/`.

New terms learned in this chapter

Let's conclude the chapter by through the new term we learned in this chapter:

- **Project automation**: A built-in tool in JWM that allows project administrators and Jira administrators to create automation rules.

Summary

In this chapter, we learned what automation in JWM is and how it can help us extend the power of JWM projects to increase productivity in our work. We learned the different components of an automation rule, how to quickly create rules from scratch, and how to use existing automation rule templates. Then, we became familiar with some common automation use cases that apply to many JWM projects and how we can replicate those rules in our own Jira instance.

With these new skills, you will be able to save time by letting automation take care of repetitive tasks and mundane work. By auto-assigning work or using auto-transitions for issue transitions, you and your coworkers will stay up to date with the status of your project.

I sincerely hope you have enjoyed your journey through this book. Keep in mind that the JWM product is still a work in progress and many new and exciting features will continue to be added in the future.

Further reading

- **Smart values**

    For more advanced work with automation rules, you will want to become familiar with **smart values**. This functionality extends your rules by applying formats to your data, use of JSON, return of multiple issues in a list, and more. You can learn about smart values here: `https://support.atlassian.com/jira-software-cloud/docs/what-are-smart-values/`.

- **Basic search functionality**

    If you are not familiar with the **Jira Query Language** (**JQL**), this article will help you learn the basics and get started immediately with searches: `https://support.atlassian.com/jira-software-cloud/docs/perform-a-basic-search/`.

- **Jira product family blog for changes**

    To help you keep track of all changes related to the JWM product, Automation, Jira software, and more, be sure to subscribe to the Jira Cloud release notes blog found here: `https://confluence.atlassian.com/cloud/blog`.

Finally, we would like to share some helpful resources you can turn to when you have problems, want to know more, or generally just have some questions.

- **Jira Work Management Cloud Support**

    This is the standard location within Atlassian's support structure to find things like documentation, suggestions and bug reports, and more. Find it all here: `https://support.atlassian.com/jira-work-management/`.

- **Atlassian User Community**

  As an Atlassian Community Leader, I would be sorely remiss if I did not encourage you to explore and join the **Atlassian Community**! The Community is designed to help all users across the Atlassian family of products. It's a place to ask questions and get helpful advice and solutions from other Atlassian users.

  And best of all, there is a dedicated space for those new to JWM. As one of the leaders for this group, I highly encourage you to take a look around, introduce yourself, and get the benefits of all things Community.

  You can access the *New to Jira Work Management* group here: `https://community.atlassian.com/t5/New-to-Jira-Work-Management/gh-p/newtojwm`.

  We will see you in the Atlassian Community!

Index

A

Appfire 95
Atlassian Marketplace apps
    JMWE 95
    reference link 96
    ScriptRunner 95
    working with 94
automation
    about 210
    rule executions 224, 225
    rules 211
    rules, creating 212-218
    templates, using 219-221
    usage limitations 224, 225
    use cases 222-224
Automation for Jira 94

B

board
    about 14, 69, 120
    components 70
    functions 72
    searching 69, 70
    second board, creating 73, 74

board configuration process
    reference link 75
board creation process
    reference link 75
Budget Creation template 37
business projects 7
business units (BUs) 5

C

Calendar
    issues, adding to 117-119
Card 49
Cloud Fortified 95
columns
    modifying 109
    order of columns, modifying 110
    resizing 110
comma-separated values (CSV) 135
components, board
    cards 71
    columns 71
    project name 71
    search and filters 71
Content Management template 27

custom fields
  about 148-152, 164
  adding, to screens 152, 153
  context, editing for 153-156
  types 148, 149

D

dashboards
  about 145
  implementing 140-144
Data Center 12
Deep Clone for Jira
  about 206, 207
  reference link 207
Document Approval template 28

E

Email Campaign template 36
email function
  about 203
  reference link 203
Extensible Markup Language (XML) 105

F

field configuration scheme 94
filters
  creating 134-137
  saving 137-139
forms
  about 120
  creating 122-124
  description, adding 126
  field labels, modifying 126-128
  fields, adding to 124, 125
  previewing 128, 129

required fields 126-128
  sharing 129, 130
functions, board
  about 72
  issue, creating 73
  issues, filtering 72
  search box 72
  status, modifying 72
functions, project workflow
  condition 86
  post function 86
  trigger 86
  validator 86

G

gadgets
  about 145
  incorporating 140-144
Gantt-style views 113
global permissions 168
go-to-market (GTM) 21
groups
  about 173
  creating 174

I

inline editable lists 68
issue layout screen 64
issue-level security
  about 192
  applying 184-189
issues
  about 64
  adding, to Calendar 117-119
  creating 49-51

creating, externally 203, 204
   viewing 130-132
issue security scheme 93
issue type scheme 93
issue type screen scheme 94
ITSM 14

J

Jira
   project types, comparing 5, 6
Jira administrator
   about 168, 191
   versus project administrator 190
Jira Cloud 12
Jira Core product
   reviewing 12
Jira Miscellaneous Workflow
      Extensions (JMWE) 95
Jira projects
   migrating, to Jira Work
      Management 204-206
Jira Query Language (JQL) 131, 211
Jira Server 12
Jira Service Management (JSM) 5, 14, 107
Jira-software-users 172
Jira Work Management (JWM)
   about 5, 14
   Administration components,
      accessing 53
   features 100
   Issue layout screen 58-61
   issue types 56, 57
   people option 56
   project details 54, 55
   schemes 62
   screens 57, 58
JSM projects 11, 12

JSW 5, 14
JSW projects
   about 8, 9
   company-managed software
      projects 9, 10
   team-managed software projects 9
JVM templates
   information, exploring 22
JVM templates, information
   board 22
   Budget Creation template 37
   Content Management template 27
   Document Approval template 28
   Email Campaign template 36
   issue types 22
   Lead Tracking template 33
   New Employee Onboarding template 31
   Performance Review template 32
   Personal Task Planner template 38
   Procurement template 34
   Project Management template 25
   Recruitment template 30
   Sales Pipeline template 35
   Task Tracking template 26
   Web Design Process template 29
   workflow 22
   workflow, reading 23, 24
JWM board
   versus, Jira software project boards 69
JWM features, relationship with issues
   about 102
   Board 102
   Calendar 102
   Forms 102
   Issues 103
   List 102
   Summary 102
   Timeline 102

JWM project administrator,
    capabilities aspects
  components 190-192
  issue layout and screens 190
  project roles 190-192
  versions and releases 190-192
  workflows 190
JWM projects
  about 7, 8, 12
  components 13, 14
  schemes 91, 92
JWM projects, tools
  Board 101
  Calendar 101
  Forms 101
  Issues 101
  List 101
  Summary 101
  Timeline 101
JWM Summary section
  about 103, 120
  activity 104-106
  statistics 106, 107
JWM templates
  about 18
  Basic Group 19
  Finance 20
  grouping 19
  Human Resources (HR) 20
  Legal 20
  Marketing/Sales 21
  Operations 21

K

Kanban 9
Kanban board 68
key 64

L

Lead Tracking template 33
list
  about 120
  columns, modifying 109
  columns, resizing 110
  filter, adding 112
  inline editing 111
  issues, sorting 113
  order of columns, modifying 110
  using 107, 108

M

Marketplace apps
  working with 206
Marketplace listing
  reference link 95
Microsoft Teams
  about 203
  reference link 203

N

New Employee Onboarding template 31
notification scheme 93

O

organization administrator 169, 191

P

People option
  free plan 176, 192
  paid plan 177, 192
Performance Review template 32

permission helper 182-184
permission scheme
  about 93, 176
  configuring 180-182
Personal Task Planner template 38
Procurement template 34
ProForma forms 122, 145
ProForma Forms 94
project
  creating 42-44
  creating, based on existing
      project 195-199
  key 45
  naming 45
  team 46
project administrator
  versus Jira administrator 190
project automation 225
project board 46, 52, 53
project details, Jira Work
      Management Administration
  avatar 55
  default assignee 55
  description 55
  key 55
  name 55
  project category 55
  project lead 55
  project type 55
  URL 55
Project Management template 25
project roles 176-179
project settings 64
project template
  about 46
  details page 44
  selecting 43

project workflow
  accessing 76, 77
  diagram view 80
  editing 82-86
  edit mode 81, 82
  functions 86
  modifying 75-77
  statuses, adding 87-91
  text view 77-79

Q

quality assurance (QA) 8
quickstart button 48
quickstart window 47, 48, 64

R

Recruitment template 30
reports
  accessing 132-134
  using 132-134
request for proposal (RFP) 20
REST API call
  about 203
  reference link 203
roadmaps 113

S

Sales Pipeline template 35
schemes 62, 64
schemes, JWM projects
  about 91, 92
  field configuration scheme 94
  issue security scheme 93
  issue type scheme 93

issue type screen scheme 94
notification scheme 93
permission scheme 93
screen scheme 93
workflow scheme 93
screens
  about 64
  custom fields, adding to 152, 153
  fields, moving between
      sections on 160-162
  schemes 162-164
  using, to edit work 156-160
  using, to view work 156-160
screen scheme 93
ScriptRunner
  about 95
  reference link 95
Scrum 9
Scrum methodology 69
shared schemes
  using 199-202
site administrator 169, 191
site-admins 172
Slack
  about 203
  reference link 203
Sprint board 68
swimlanes 22

T

Task Tracking template 26
team-managed projects 14
template
  usage, deciding 39
timeline
  about 120
  dependencies 115, 116

durations, modifying 114
exporting 116
filters 116
sharing 117
working with 113, 114
transitions 78
two-dimensional (2D) 140

U

Uniform Resource Locator
      (URL) 117, 123
user list 172, 173
user management 168-172

W

watchers 104
Web Design Process template 29
workflows 62, 63
workflow scheme 93

`Packt.com`

Subscribe to our online digital library for full access to over 7,000 books and videos, as well as industry leading tools to help you plan your personal development and advance your career. For more information, please visit our website.

Why subscribe?

- Spend less time learning and more time coding with practical eBooks and Videos from over 4,000 industry professionals

- Improve your learning with Skill Plans built especially for you

- Get a free eBook or video every month

- Fully searchable for easy access to vital information

- Copy and paste, print, and bookmark content

Did you know that Packt offers eBook versions of every book published, with PDF and ePub files available? You can upgrade to the eBook version at `packt.com` and as a print book customer, you are entitled to a discount on the eBook copy. Get in touch with us at `customercare@packtpub.com` for more details.

At `www.packt.com`, you can also read a collection of free technical articles, sign up for a range of free newsletters, and receive exclusive discounts and offers on Packt books and eBooks.

Other Books You May Enjoy

If you enjoyed this book, you may be interested in these other books by Packt:

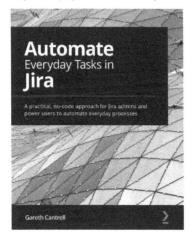

Automate Everyday Tasks in Jira

Gareth Cantrell

ISBN: 9781800562868

- Understand the basic concepts of automation such as triggers, conditions, and actions
- Find out how to use if–then scenarios and conditions to automate your processes with practical examples
- Use smart values to achieve complex and more powerful automation
- Implement use cases in a practical way, including automation with Slack, Microsoft Teams, GitHub, and Bitbucket
- Discover best practices for writing and maintaining automation rules
- Explore techniques for debugging rules and solving common issues

Scaling Agile with Jira Align

Dean MacNeil, Aslam Cader

ISBN: 9781800203211

- Understand Jira Align's key factors for success
- Find out how you can connect people, work, time, and outcomes with Jira Align
- Navigate and collaborate in Jira Align
- Scale team agility to the portfolio and enterprise
- Delve into planning and execution, including roadmaps and predictability metrics
- Implement lean portfolio management and OKRs
- Get to grips with handling bimodal and hybrid delivery
- Enable advanced data security and analytics in Jira Align

Packt is searching for authors like you

If you're interested in becoming an author for Packt, please visit `authors.packtpub.com` and apply today. We have worked with thousands of developers and tech professionals, just like you, to help them share their insight with the global tech community. You can make a general application, apply for a specific hot topic that we are recruiting an author for, or submit your own idea.

Share Your Thoughts

Now you've finished *Jira Work Management for Business Teams*, we'd love to hear your thoughts! Scan the QR code below to go straight to the Amazon review page for this book and share your feedback or leave a review on the site that you purchased it from.

`https://packt.link/r/1803232005`

Your review is important to us and the tech community and will help us make sure we're delivering excellent quality content.

www.ingramcontent.com/pod-product-compliance
Lightning Source LLC
Chambersburg PA
CBHW060537060326
40690CB00017B/3526